MORPHEUS UNCHAINED

Remembrances

of a Future Dream

W. E. GUTMAN

CCB Publishing
British Columbia, Canada

Morpheus Unchained: Remembrances of a Future Dream

Non-fiction. Essays. Politics. Ontology.

Copyright ©2016 by W. E. Gutman
ISBN-13   978-1-77143-272-6
First Edition

Library and Archives Canada Cataloguing in Publication
Gutman, W. E., 1937-, author
Morpheus unchained : remembrances of a future dream
/ written by W. E. Gutman. -- First edition.
Issued in print and electronic formats.
ISBN 978-1-77143-272-6 (pbk.).--ISBN 978-1-77143-273-3 (pdf)
Additional cataloguing data available from Library and Archives Canada

Cover design by the author.

Cover background: Grey paper texture: © valkot | Canstockphoto.com

This book is printed on acid-free paper.

Extreme care has been taken by the author to ensure that all information presented in this book is accurate and up to date at the time of
publishing. The publisher cannot be held responsible for any errors or
omissions. Additionally, neither is any liability assumed by the publisher for damages resulting from the use of the information contained
herein.

Publisher: CCB Publishing
                    British Columbia, Canada
                    www.ccbpublishing.com

Contents

*There is no document of civilization which
is not at the same time a document of barbarism.*
Walter Benjamin (1892-1940)

Man was born free, and he is everywhere in chains.
Jean-Jacques Rousseau (1712-1778)

*The only way to deal with an unfree world
is to become so absolutely free that your very
existence is an act of rebellion.*
Albert Camus (1913-1960)

HISTORY: ECHO AND WARNING

In 2015, a team of archeologists from the Czech Institute of Egyptology, Charles University, Prague, unearthed the tomb of a Pharaonic queen who ruled Egypt's Old Kingdom four and a half millennia ago. This era marked the beginning of a series of dynamics and events that would threaten and eventually lay waste to the Old Kingdom. Nepotism, greed, the destabilizing role of special interest groups, corruption, reckless alliances, wars, and climate change coalesced to bring an end not only to Egypt's Old Kingdom but concurrently to other advanced societies in the Middle East and Europe.

Within two centuries of the queen's death, the Nile ceased flooding and drought spread across the land, leading to the dissolution of the age of the pyramid builders. Without abundant floods, harvests were stunted and taxes could not be levied, making it difficult to finance the governing apparatus and sustain the belief system and integrity of the realm.

◆

Four thousand years later, between the 8th and 9th century of the Common Era, a similar set of influences contributed to the collapse of the once mighty Maya empire.

The Maya feared death more than any of life's ordeals, and only exceptional individuals, they claimed, could find their way to the heavenly gates. The unworthy were hastily dispatched to *Xibalba,* the Maya hell, the "House of Gloom," the "World of Ghosts, the "Mansion of the Damned," an icy abyss teeming with monsters that inflict unspeakable torments. If the Maya took great pains to elude the dreaded chasm — self-mutilation and orgiastic human sacrifices, they believed, could forestall the inevitable — they had no illusion that life "on the surface" was apt to be as hideous as in *Xibalba's* entrails. Ego, avarice, unspeakable cruelty and violence, deception and vengeance, all prevailed, acted out with an incontinence bordering on lunacy. Blood-lettings, skirmishes, ceremonial decapitations and amputations, in short, senseless carnage, were as likely to envenom their mortal exist-ence as the "lower regions" to which their souls would eventually be consigned.

Longing for redemption, fearing night, awaiting dawn but not the passage of greater events, their governors pandered to unfeeling gods and offered sacrifices to atone inexpiable sins while the masses were fated to a life of submission and servitude in the shadow of despotic and degenerate elites. Busy erecting flamboyant pantheons, obsessed with their own place in posterity, the nihilistic demi-gods the people idolized were no kinder that the bloodthirsty Lords of *Xibalba*. They knew they were false of heart, promoters of evil and tormentors of men, and that their extrava-gance and folly would lead to civil strife, so-cial disintegration, economic exhaustion, and, in due course, apocalypse.

Eventually, the debauchery, the drug-induced stupor, the bombastic mystique of their masters' esoteric pursuits began to wear thin in the eyes of the overburdened populace. Too long had the commoners been forced into a life of servitude; too onerous was the endless labor involved in erecting temples, sacrificial altars, and ball courts. They were tired of tending the fields of the princely castes and paying exorbitant tributes to crooked and insensitive monarchs. For centuries the multitudes had surrendered to the ruling aristocracy and soon the sting of despotism, the ignominy of persecution would lead to open revolt.

Along with the sharp increase in the dominance of privileged classes and the unfettered opulence and ostentation their lifestyle demanded, the number of underlings required to cater to their whims grew exponentially. This imposed additional burdens for food and other goods needed to support the nobility. It is likely that these liabilities triggered ever-widening rifts and fed mounting hostilities between the populace and their masters.

There is evidence in the Late Classic era, the period foreshadowing the "fall," of a population explosion that led to the growth in the number and size of urban clusters. All these pressures — overpopulation, soaring demand for goods and services, shrinking resources and spreading divisions among the people— had a profound impact on the Maya: It left them teetering on the brink. Mortally wounded, nudged by an irresistible momentum, the once great, the magnificent Maya empire quivered, froze and dipped over the edge.

The precise undercurrents that led to the Maya's sudden and staggering collapse are not well understood. What is known is that famine, brought on by deforestation, over-cultivation, climatic fluctuations, floods followed by protracted droughts, the outbreak of infectious diseases, rising infant mortality, declining life expectancy, and widespread discontent with an increasingly remote and self-absorbed plutocracy, led to chaos, fragmentation and dispersal. All are the consequences of a system of governance rigged to benefit the few at the expense of the many in an epoch, not unlike our own, when disaster struck and irreversible ruination ensued.

For the surviving full-blooded Maya— some four million live in Belize, Guatemala and Honduras—only two paths of survival are left: serfdom and assimilation, or alternating states of neglect and violent repression by the gatecrashers who now occupy their domain. They remain suspended between two contrasting and incongruous worlds: ancient (intimate and familiar) and modern (alien and menacing).

Sooner or later, plutocratic rule and the debaucheries to which free enterprise must resort in order to prevail invite anarchy.

The past is prologue.

A CUMBERSOME NECESSITY

There are many truths.
There is a truth for every being and for every particle of
the universe. Each one reflects its discoverer in a differ-
ent way. To seek the truth means more than finding
your own. It means finding a truth that works for you
and for the other guy, for now and forever, in this place
and everywhere, for the body and for the soul, for the
sage and for the neophyte. The higher the truth, the few-
er boundaries it knows.
Rabbi Menachem Mendel Schneerson (1902-1994)

The first challenge a writer faces is finding the context in which to articulate the things he wants to say. I always knew that my calling was to give verbal expression to the truth but I also sensed that the truth, whether lobbed like a grenade or swaddled in tactful imagery is, to a vast number of people, insufferable. The blaming game began in high school when, annoyed by what they called "youthful bluster" (I was just playing devil's advocate) teachers urged me to "tone down the rhetoric." Later, I earned high grades for style and the censure of college professors wearied by my "Jacobin oratory." Later yet (I was now an impecunious journalist), many of my columns routinely elicited scorching feedbacks from readers. On two occasions (I was working in Central America at the time) I received death threats for divulging truths that a local journalist warned, "are best left untold." I remember accusing him of abdicating his professional duties.

"When your job is done," he reminded me tartly, "you go back to your country where you're safe, whereas I live here."

"That's true," I conceded, "in which case you might want to consider another occupation."

My iconoclasm has always put me in vulnerable but intellectually exhilarating positions. Leaving readers wondering to what ends I will go to flush out the truth or how far my irreverence will take me, are inexhaustible founts of inspiration and euphoria.

The question is not whether telling the truth can cause harm — it will on occasion, not more so than a lie, I always retort — but whether there is an obligation to unearth and expose it; whether withholding it, especially where freedom, justice and civil liberties are endangered (say, when governments snoop on their citizens, lie to them, exploit them, kidnap them, capriciously suspend habeas corpus, and torture them) will do irreparable damage. The jury is deadlocked but the proverbial High Bench of public opinion, rarely a weatherglass of mainstream attitudes, continues to rule in favor of silence in the face of untruths: Asking too many questions, "stirring the pot," "making waves," "rocking the boat," upsetting the status quo, I'm being repeatedly warned, is tantamount to treason. Some people routinely accuse me of siding with the devil, of flirting with sedition. I remorselessly do what I can to prove them right. As I write elsewhere, "To be credible, the truth can't afford to be harmless."

♦

Published in 2015, *Morpheus Possessed,* which the following work finds itself awkwardly compelled to revisit, speaks of an odd and contentious truth: the conflict between dream and reality. In it, unrepentantly flaunting some of my most disquieting visions (I'd corralled a herd of errant phantasms and memorialized their gossamer existence in a notebook lest they shrivel in the dustbin of oblivion), I ask: Do we dream the life we live? Or are we the misshapen relics of someone else's depraved imagination? Are the memories we hoard along the way mere mental scaffoldings lacking tangible actuality? If life is a lucid dream, is reality the toxic mirror image of the dreams we weave? I left the questions largely unanswered. I was hoping readers would ponder these ambiguities on their won. When we cease to dream, I asserted in the concluding chapter, "all we *are* ceases to be. Everything else is a tawdry cliché." I wasn't referring to nocturnal flights of fancy.

The book was not well received. It may have been misread because it was either miswritten (it hid behind parables to advance ideas that need no symbolic garnish to be understood); or it was lavished on readers who have no flair for lyricism, no taste for allegory, no appetite for complex ideas. I'd ignored one of the fundamental lessons taught in journalism school: Don't philosophize. Know your audience. Keep it simple; aim at the lowest common denominator. Deliver the truth like an uppercut and narrow your stance...." I had used a scented feather duster instead of a blackjack.

◆

Armed with the best of intentions, a handful of readers wrote to say how much they had enjoyed the book. To my dismay, they never spelled out what they liked about it. Their encomiums were peppered with formulaic niceties, yet it was obvious that they had failed to grasp the deeper insights this diminutive opus had been crafted to impart. Enticed by the images I painted, they were not roused by the reformist ideas the images conveyed. They took things literally. Nor did they heed my advice: Do not attempt to deconstruct dreams. Parsing a dream, I cautioned—much like explicating an abstract painting—diminishes it, trivializes it. Some inventoried their dreams, perhaps in the vain hope that I might help decipher them. Others showered me with thanks for making them "feel at ease" about their dreams. Their accolades were disappointing but I did not resent their inability to relate: Not everyone dreams. Few recall the spectral abyss into which they are sucked as they surrender to sleep. Fewer know how to erect a coherent narrative of the visions that visit them; fewer still attribute any significance to, let alone derive any creative inspiration from, their nocturnal escapades. None of these gentle critics ventured beyond the graphic nature of the dream sequences I detailed in the book. None was able to distill from their metaphorical complexion the greater underlying message: Society, instead of refining humans, corrupts them. The dream of liberty, the abolition of empire, the elimination of masters and rulers, in short, the freedom to live under a law of one's own enactment is the dream that humankind must transmute into irrevocable reality. For too long, I had hinted, happiness had consisted of living life reflexively, disregarding its absurdity while self-crowned overlords imposed order on existence and self-anointed moral arbiters forced their subjects to seek answers to unanswerable questions in rigid, cruel, often farcical beliefs. I had written:

"Limitless and everlasting, the world of dreams is a dimension where inhibitions and scruples are left at the door. It's the flip side of a reality vigilantly managed by dissimilar but tactically congruent interests whose reciprocal aim is to restrain the errant ways of radicals and non-conformists—of dreamers. Awake, we are condemned to be free but arbitrary laws, a shadowy judicial machine that grinds us to a pulp, synthetic social covenants, rigid customs and traditions, the prying eyes and ears of a paranoid political sovereignty and the hypocrisy of the rabble, repeatedly overturn our sentence. Conscious, we live in a realm where no crime, however odious, can be committed without the consent of the perpetrator and the loud applause of silent accomplices. Conscious, we are under constant scrutiny. Asleep, we are under no obligation to conform. We can surrender to our basest instincts, defy authority, settle scores, and roam unhindered as far as our imagination—or dream-induced psychoses—will take us."

In my haste to telegraph what I believe are axiomatic truths, and much to my regret, I surrendered to the esotericism of crystal gazing instead of the sweeping, "take no prisoners" dialectic of anarchy found in my other writings. I was evidently preaching to a very small choir of like-minded mutineers while multitudes of old-line believers, absorbed in their numbing devotions, deprived of voluntary movement (and incapable of independent thinking), sat in their pews, fixated on the wacky, morbid, salacious and psychotic dreams I bawdily paraded in *Morpheus Possessed*. These good people were so caught up in their affectations that they couldn't see "the forest for the trees." In short, I had foolishly contrived to arouse an audience that could only be stirred by the delirium, prurience, and incongruities with which my dreams were drenched, not by what they inferred.

Last, complicit in the unintentional misrepresentations that impart *Morpheus Possessed* with a character it doesn't possess (or an aim it never claimed to have), thus leading countless readers astray, is the publishing industry's fixation on taxonomy—classifying books by "genre." While *Morpheus Possessed* irrefutably uses dreams as metaphors for reality (and vice-versa), it is **not** and never was meant to be a "body, mind, spirit, self-help" guide into the mystical realm of dreams, as it was classified. I am not a mystic. I don't have what it takes to be one. I never will. As for metaphors,

I carelessly indulged in them because they helped me translate deeply abstract concepts into tangible ideas. Abstractions are of little interest to contemporary readers. They are driven by stimuli, not introspection. They don't want to be roused into states of self-awareness; reality is just too much to bear.

◆

There is nothing spiritual or supernatural about reality, less yet about dreams. What I sought to do, clumsily disregarding a large chunk of the reading public, was to advance a simple if bewildering proposition: Dreams are not only sublime "fruits" that grow in the obscure, inaccessible and bountiful orchard of the *id*, but that, owing their spontaneity and mercurial nature, they are the purest expression of an intuitive freedom that transcends immateriality, that strives toward tangible physicality. I further tried to convey the notion that the freedom to dream has nothing to do with the errant ghosts that populate our slumber but rather that we must vigorously protect the freedoms we enjoy in our wakeful state from those who might deny us the right to govern our lives—freedom from an antidemocratic, neo-feudal gerontocracy that sends the young to die on distant battlefields and a money-grubbing gentry bent on robotizing the minds and bodies of a new generation of peons. For what is a free man, I asked, but one who has the freedom to rule himself?

I failed.

The apologia that follows is not an afterthought but an elaboration on the lies, injustices and desecrations warily outlined in *Morpheus Possessed*. Instead of a romp in the minefields of REM sleep, *Morpheus Unchained* is about dreams (as in wishes, longings, hopes and objectives, as well as in false dreams, broken dreams, deceptive dreams, recurring dreams, premonitory dreams, impossible dreams and living nightmares). It more forcefully argues that being dependent on—or compelled to submit to—someone else's dreams (laws, policies, edicts and injunctions) is slavery, whereas freedom (which is inseparable from justice) means having no sovereign—earthly or heavenly. To be free, I hasten to say, we need to seek in history a rationale for what looms as a very uncertain future. We must beware of people who subordinate reality to fantasy, who preach neutrality, who speak of "addressing both sides of an issue," who advocate laissez-faire, who promote "conflict resolution" and "national reconciliation" while ignoring the legitimate claims of the victims of state-sponsored evil. They are not interested in justice or truth. What they want is to force appeasements and extract concessions contrived to thwart the kind of upheavals that the pursuit, discovery, and airing of inconvenient truths ignite.

Does any of this matter? Have my lifelong wrangles with inertia, dogmatism and mediocrity in any way advanced the cause of truth? I cannot think of a single instance in which they did — save a few milliseconds of frothing rage leveled at me by readers who call themselves patriots and grant themselves the right to harangue under the cloak of anonymity.

The following essays, each suggestive of the myriad dilemmas that challenge dreamers, point in one direction: This is a war. Mankind must militate toward a realm — I call it a *Dreamdom* — in which the dream, at last, takes over so that we may one day embark on the grandest dream of all, the one near-life experience from which we need never awaken: Freedom from the tyranny of inflexible beliefs, freedom from a demagoguery that mirrors the affluent, genteel minority's tradition of scape-

goating others in order to maintain its authority. What obstacles must be overcome to ensure
safe passage is the subject of this heretofore-
unintended sequel.

THE RIGHT TO DREAM

Dreams are intensely personal but they all have one thing in common: They're the undigested or disfigured leftovers of subconscious musings, the echoes of unresolved issues that preoccupy or torment us when we're awake. Where they differ is the manner in which they are construed. We are not all knitted from the same skein. Instead, we are the sum total of convergent and cumulative influences: heredity, upbringing and education. If we're lucky, only our genes betray us. Some of us are marked by events that indelibly alter our *élan vital*, the life force that animates us. How we might have turned out had these intervening ordeals spared us is anyone's guess. Thus, we process our nightly visitations in ways that reflect our ethnicity, culture, religion (or lack thereof), the idioms in which we communicate (people who speak different tongues reason differently), and the social milieu in which we evolve.

Superficial differences aside, no two dreams are alike. Australian aborigines speak of the "Dreamtime" in terms and imageries that elude western thought. Likewise, my dreams, which reflect anxieties common to my realm and epoch, and replicate concepts, sounds, and situations familiar to modern man, will seem risible, demented or frightening to these living relics of prehistory.

Freud suggests that dreams are an expression of repressed hankerings.

To Hindus, dreams are real and brought on by the Supreme Brahman. They can either be oracular or punitive.

Buddhists do not consider dreams to be fantasies, but rather symbols of the illusions of our everyday experience of life.

The Maya believed that dreams contain secret codes shared by other people, both alive and dead who, like the angels of the Bible, impart new knowledge to the dreamer.

Ancient Egyptians held dreams in high esteem. To them, dreaming was an excursion into the underworld. The journey could be fraught with dangers, but it could also be rewarding. They could communicate with the gods, peer into the future, do magic or heal illnesses while dreaming. They also believed it was possible to project nightmares onto their enemies.

Sikhism, a religion of love, peace, and classless parity, suggests that the world itself is a dream, that people find no peace in their dreams; they sleep immersed in pain.

According to the Kabbalah, the soul leaves the body when we sleep and ascends to its heavenly source to replenish its energy. While a residue of the soul remains with the body to keep it alive, the main portion of the soul travels to higher places. In this disembodied state, the soul is free to experience visions and happenstances that are usually off-limits to beings of this world. This includes the possibility of meeting other disembodied souls — particularly the souls of loved ones who have passed away — perhaps even a dybbuk.[1]

Figurative language aside, the nexus that underlies our humanity — that of the naked bushman who roams the outback and the three-piece-suited executive who gazes at the world from a thirty-story skyscraper window — is (a) the effect that the disconnection between hallucination and "conscious" existence has on the psyche; and (b) the subtle if persistent sensation that we are never quite as free as when we dream. It is a freedom, in the literal and figurative, that must at all cost be defended. We *are* what we dream.

◆

While serious researchers seek to understand the subconscious mind, and charlatans defraud gullible souls by "reading" their dreams and charting their future, dreaming, an occupation that can be understood as *aspiring, hankering, hoping* and *yearning,* is more often put to use in the service of greed, lust, ambition, narcissism, and self-promotion.

---

[1] *A dybbuk is the spirit of a dead person who has escaped from Gehenna (the Jewish purgatory) and who attaches itself to another person on earth. According to Kabbalistic tradition, a soul that was unable to fulfill its destiny when alive is given another chance to do so in the form of a dybbuk.*

As I reminisce in *Morpheus Possessed*, "my dream," one my classmates declared, "is to become a famous battlefield commander." The son of a business tycoon dreamed "of being a millionaire." There was a wannabe cowboy, a strange desire for a city boy whose only exposure to horses was astride the wooden equines at the neighborhood merry-go-round. Other boys dreamed of becoming a gendarme, a Michelin-star-aspiring chef. Another sought movie stardom; another yet craved the adulation of adoring fans on soccer stadia. There wasn't a single budding poet, storyteller, artist or musician, no star-gazer, no would-be philosopher, explorer, seafarer or entomologist, no humanist, no mystic, no enlightened reformer, only uninspired little pragmatists and one lone, starry-eyed pigtailed romantic who mistook hope for fait accompli by imagining – *dreaming* – "a better world, a world without conflict."

One is not born greedy. Greed is an acquired taste sweetened by moral decay.

♦

There burns bright in the pit of all men's hearts, from Tokyo to Timbuktu, Jerusalem to

Jenin, Shanghai to Sao Paolo, irrespective of race or religious persuasion, one timeless, universal dream: Freedom from foreign occupation, repression and persecution; freedom from ethnic and religious intolerance; freedom to worship gods and freedom to reject all divinities and creeds; freedom from a sordid system of power, privilege and patronage that turns the planet into a filthy and evil-smelling imperialist encampment; freedom from fiscal policies that benefit only the wealthy; freedom from want, hunger and homelessness; freedom to live and die in peace in an economy where price controls on all but the most extravagant commodities make basic necessities affordable to everyone, where the seller must beware, not the buyer, and where gun-toting Neanderthals with an axe to grind are disarmed and their weapons are turned into plowshares.

TO SEEK [KNOWLEDGE] IS TO *KNOW*

I began to dream as soon as I learned to read. Hans Christian Andersen, Lewis Carroll, La Fontaine, the Brothers Grimm, and Charles Perrault gave my nascent imagination wings. Bucolic or eerie, inspiring, moralistic or scary, their tales fed an early urge to "know" beyond the words. They also helped awaken the perception, hazy at first, soon clearer and terrifying, that the world is a complicated place, that men are paradoxical creatures given as much to hatred as to love, conceit as to modesty, greed as to generosity, cruelty as to compassion, treachery as to loyalty, that life is a ceaseless struggle for man and beast, that there are more witches than good fairies, and that not all stories have a happy ending.

As the Second World War thundered across the globe, and drawing parallels between imaginary miscreants and real villains, I soon realized that the ogres who lurk in a child's dreams do come out of the shadows to quench their bloodlust. Nine-tenths of my family perished in Hitler's extermination factories. What Hitler could not achieve, Stalin endeavored to finish, with equally monstrous results. Dreaming, I quickly understood, needed to shift from involuntary and random expeditions to the farthest reaches of the psyche to a conscious manifestation of deliberate will. It was in books that I would continue to seek—and find—some elemental answers. I needed to fashion a personal ethos, to develop a code that would both embody and feed an embryonic but increasingly clearer optic of the world around me. Long periods of aimless globetrotting would help shed light on the organic blanks that books alone can't fill in.

◆

After several years of forced itinerancy in

post-war-torn Europe, I returned to Paris, my hometown, and enrolled at the *École Supérieure de Journalisme*. Tucked away at the end of a narrow five-story wooden staircase was home, sweet home. It was in the nurturing silence of this sparsely furnished mansard that I withdrew after school. I'd hasten to the dormer, part the chintz curtains and gape at my city the way a boy covets a woman. Below were the streets. I could read in their cadence like from an open diary, and I reveled at their pantomimes. Paris spread before me, a tapestry of gilded domes, verdant parks, wide esplanades, and ancient spires, and I'd marvel at their loveliness long after twilight had draped the City of Light in a star-studded mantle of lilac and periwinkle blue.

I'd then turn to my books. In their pages, I explored the unrevealed nature of things, unearthing strange and wondrous emotions, toying with enticing abstractions. I wanted to conquer everything that is known and, if possible, to reconnoiter all that is unknowable. All-consuming as it was, such quest, I would soon discover, was in vain. Curiosity is a long hallway with an infinite number of doors. Most can never be unlocked. I'd find consolation by telling myself that to *seek* knowledge is to *know*. In prospecting the unknown, I would also concede that I was less interested in acquiring new knowledge than in how revealed knowledge played on my imagination, how it sparked the dreams. Once digested, essential knowledge and fresh perspectives opened up a world into which I withdrew the better to savor the transcendent realms they evoked. I was intent, at all cost, and with each newly apprehended truth, to let the dreams roam free. Knowledge was in vain unless it had the capacity to stir, touch, shock, stupefy, enthrall, and kindle other dreams. The totality of all knowledge, I resolved, must culminate in action.

Surrealism, still in vogue in post-war Paris, played a pivotal role in this frenetic self-scrutiny. The eccentric cultural movement of the 1920s might have eluded me altogether had I not heard it dismissed as "intellectual snobbery," "spiritual degeneracy," and a "hoax perpetrated by petty artists bent on scandalizing the purist mainstream." Criticism of an idea, more so than praise, tends to pique my interest. It might even gain my support. "Purism is pedantry; mainstream is mundane," I would protest.

Distracting society from its utilitarian yoke

and reconciling irrationality with the rigors of conscious thought—a fundamental aim of Surrealism—found immediate favor with the wayward, non-conformist I was destined to be. The works I read, the avant-garde paintings, sculptures, films, and musical compositions I discovered along the way, produced an immediate and lasting "high." I still chuckle whenever I listen to Igor Stravinsky's *Le Sacre du Printemps* (The Rite of Spring). The nihilistic ballet caused a near-riot when it was first performed in Paris in 1913. While delighting young progressive spectators, the atonal music and salacious choreography scandalized a mostly black-tie conservative audience allergic to artistic eccentricity.

It was Charles Baudelaire, one of France's most revered literary icons, who introduced me to a new world of dreams. The formidable French bard lavished not only the exquisite harmony of his stanzas on a young, hungry mind; read with quasi-liturgical fervor, his *Les Fleurs du Mal* also seemed to legitimize and vindicate my most visceral inclinations. Trusting neither man nor God, Baudelaire takes refuge in primal chaos, in the flesh, in orgiastic sin. His verses crawl with monsters and freaks and pitiable *demi-monde* creatures all too reminiscent of ourselves. He awakens our demons, the ghouls that doze or stir within us, those we can never disavow. Shunned and lonely, he found redemption in the anonymity of crowds, among beggars, harlots, drunkards.

Whereas we are conditioned to regard ugliness as a blasphemy, as an offense by nature against innocence and vulnerability, as an unwanted gift by an uncaring donor to an unwilling recipient, Baudelaire does not see cripples — physical or emotional — as pathetic and pitiable creatures affronted by their creator, but as mythic beings and instruments of divine strategy. He finds lyricism in their disfigurement, inspiration in their tragic uniqueness. He walks among creatures that endure life's brutality and anticipate death with courage and dignity. He reminds the unmindful and the cynic that we all need someone smaller, weaker than we are, that the poor, the cripple, the simple-minded, the sinners often teach valuable lessons in bravery and nobility to the well-to-do, the unimpaired, the worldly. In sad or worn faces, he discovers traces of fathomless drama; in ephemeral smiles he sees a twinkling of hope deferred. His is the voice of all who love unrequitedly, who suffer inconsolably, who savor rare joys with stirring intensity, and who endure the sorrows, the longings and broken dreams that clutter the deepest regions of our being. He drowns his rage and agonizing melancholy in alcohol and opium, and he dies at forty-six, having exhausted all his dreams.

◆

If Arthur Rimbaud and Edgar Allan Poe (Baudelaire's contemporaries and partners-in-rhyme) gave madness a lyrical hue, it was Jean Cocteau, France's alchemical man, who urged me up the spiral stairway of surrealist dreams, who shepherded me across its portals and eased me into its wondrous inner sanctum. I gamboled and drowsed with Cocteau in fragrant fields of poppy only to awaken sprinting in place in a relay race against myself. Forever seeking to jolt men out of their torpor as he himself prowls at the edges of delirium and paranoia, Cocteau's trails are strewn with mockery for the zealot, scorn toward the hypocrite, disdain for the uninspired, and dark, seething pity for banality. Now and again I set sail on the wings of his allegories just to keep in shape. Every time I alight from these fantastic voyages I am reminded that rationality is no match for intuitiveness; that the imponderable can be hinted at only by appealing to the imagination, not common sense. No, dreamers do not live in ivory towers. Instead, they take careful aim, topple these flimsy abode and scatter their debris for all to see. Once fathomed, dreams encourage dreamers to seek within themselves new dimensions, hidden planes of awareness. Dreaming is the language of free spirits, the idiom of free thought.

Disquieting as my enthusiasm for Surrealism might have seemed (I would exploit this perceived eccentricity to discomfit those who were vexed by it), and in spite of a growing interest in the abstruse, I was still very much a boy of eighteen and, like all French boys, I devoured Alexandre Dumas. In the flip of a page I became D'Artagnan and Edmond Dantès and Joseph Balsamo. I wooed fair maidens and rode dashing steeds in pursuit of knaves and miscreants. I fought desperate duels on the side of the just, against tyrants, scheming aristocrats and perfidious clergy. I escaped from dungeons, eluded the gallows, exposed dastardly cabals, and restored the good and the righteous to their rightful stations.

Mark Twain's landscapes and perspectives evoked settings and locales of an America now long gone, and of mores and prejudices that, shockingly, still persist. Wanderlust and a craving for the hinterlands of exoticism would be further whetted by Joseph Conrad, James Fenimore Cooper, Jack London, Pierre Loti, Herman Melville, James Michener, Marco Polo, Robert Louis Stevenson, and Jules Verne, to name a few.

Often, perhaps too often (some friends and relatives regarded my fondness for the bizarre and nightmarish a "malignancy") I'd turn to Franz Kafka the conjurer, Kafka, *the supreme fabulist of modern's man's cosmic predicament,"* for booster shots of cynicism, the serum that protects dreamers from tyrannical falsities, from the bleak fancies of diehards and ob-structionists. I meandered without haste in his miasmic labyrinths, eager to get lost, willing to become ensnared in his inscrutable plots, to merge into them. Kafka would inoculate me against the meanness of human stupidity, the absurdity, the despotism of officialdom, the odious banality of bureaucracy, the effrontery and intolerance of the know-nothings, the shallow intellect and miserly preoccupations of the petty bourgeoisie, the boorishness and vulgarity of the rabble, the sham majesty of the privileged classes.

Hardened by experience and an ebbing regard for all authority, these aversions would be reinforced by Friedrich Nietzsche's warnings against mindless dictates. What I gained from his florid orations was the courage to dismember the tentacles of absurdity, dogma and prejudice (Moses Maimonides called them, "degenerate practices and senseless beliefs.") Oh, how I struggled with Nietzsche. But I read on and reread *The Antichrist, Ecce Homo, Twilight of the Gods,* and *Thus Spoke Zarathustra,* and I agonized over every thought, every last convoluted paragraph. And I was changed forever.

From Baruch Spinoza, I learned to reject doctrines that don't make room for speculation or doubt. I began to call a lie any "truth" that owes its existence solely to blind faith. Shackled to unbending creeds, afflicted with intellectual villainy, his contemporaries shunned and rebuked him. Excommunicated by his fellow Jews (as was Maimonides), vilified by Christians, he was the superb heretic I aspired to be. His was an enviable malediction, I mused, and I remember vowing to emulate him in some way. It would take a more mature perusal of his work to recognize that I lacked both his formidable intellect and his tact. I would have to settle for the heretic's willingness to invite hostility. In one of my less contentious college essays, I wrote,

> *"Men struggle and fight. They're so busy fooling themselves so they might weather what is unbearable that they'd rather live with lies than the truth. In attempting to rationalize mirages, they dupe others along the way."*

François-Marie Arouet (Voltaire), the freethinker whose moral code hinged on tolerance, was also required reading. Hostile to all metaphysics, Voltaire cautions against the perils of immoderation with sardonic ferocity. A believer in "natural religion" — deism — he condemns the social effects of "revealed" tenets, calling them "pernicious," thus earning him the unwavering and irrevocable enmity of the Church. There can be no higher proof of one's relevance in a world of staggering hypocrisy, I thought, than to attract such antagonism. Convinced that it is more useful to be hated than ignored, I fantasized that my writings would one day be listed, along with those of other satirists and "irreligious libertines," in the *Index Librorum Prohibitorium*. Alas, such accolade has so far eluded me. Instead, I now take comfort in the near-certainty that a tight-lipped but all-knowing Big Brother is keeping me in his sights.

George Orwell's view of freedom — "the right to tell people what they don't want to know" — appealed to me intuitively. But it was the stirring humanism of Victor Hugo and Emile Zola, their attention to the unlearned lessons of history, which steeled my resolve to "tell," to startle the smug and the compliant, to challenge the established order, to forecast chaos and decay as a hedge against their inevitability. Hugo and Zola celebrated the enormous power of passionate, hard-hitting reportage, the poetry of polemic, the elegance of words honed to sing and sting and move men to great deeds and, occasionally, to drive them to infamy, shame and remorse. Those whose sole loyalty is to the truth, I would eventually realize, have very few friends. I would for a time revel in the vainglorious illusion that being friendless is a small price to pay for ferreting the truth — smaller yet for stripping it naked for all to see. Alienation, jobs lost or denied, opportunities forfeited and, later, threats from some very irate readers, did little to tame the craving. These hindrances taught me to modulate the rhetoric, not to curb it. I would also learn that the "truth" is often the strongest or most persuasively defended assumption—not an unassailable verity—and that the urge by some to exhume it is habitually frustrated by those who want to keep it entombed.

◆

All my mentors were there at my beck and call, lovingly shelved in alphabetical order, ready to impart fresh insights, to titillate, amuse and exhort, astound and inspire at every turn of the page. They kept me company when homework was done, or postponed, as I waited for the girls to climb to my old drafty garret, eager to regale them with recitations from Guillaume Apollinaire's erotic novellas, and the Marquis de Sade's most salacious prose.

It was in the sagacity of books, in their wit and nonconformity that I trusted most. And it was in their company that I withdrew long after the girls had gone home and that carnal lust, for now appeased, yielded to more cerebral cravings and to the greater dividends of sleep, alone at last, in my very narrow bed as I surrendered to night.

THE CHILD OF MY GREATEST PAIN

I'd rather live without hope than nourish a dream that can never be, I mused as the curtain came down and theater patrons snaked through the aisles toward the lobby during intermission to stretch their legs, wet their whistles, empty their bladders, grab a smoke and talk over each other until the buzz of several hundred voices crested to an incoherent drone.

Swedish playwright August Strindberg's tragedy, *A Dream Play*, argues that "human beings are pitiable;" that "every joy must be paid twice over with sorrow;" and that humanity's only reality is the endless repetition of "duty and sin and guilt." I was fifteen when my parents took me to see this strange and troubling drama. I remember how stunned I was to discover that the same insights, doubts, fears, and antipathies awakened in me at an early age by a succession of life-altering ordeals had been so vividly rendered, more than three decades before I was born, not in a work of philosophy or a morality play but in a stage production created to tell the world that life is an illusion and that dreams can never be fulfilled.

Written in 1901, the play takes audiences on an anguished journey into the unconscious mind. Foreshadowing the anxieties, misgivings, and horrors that would soon engulf the world, it nimbly echoes some of the convulsions, obscenities and crimes that disgraced and bloodied the pages of history in the decade preceding the dawn of a new century. Surely, Strindberg must have been mindful of these upheavals as he devised the plot and gave his characters their wraithlike existence:

☞ General Fiorenzo Bava-Beccaris orders troops to fire on a rally in Milan. Eighty people are killed; hundreds are injured. Italy's King Umberto I, who hailed the massacre, is assassinated.

❧ Alleging state-sponsored anti-Semitism, and charging the government of conspiring to imprison French Army captain Alfred Dreyfus, a Jew falsely accused of treason, novelist Émile Zola's blistering editorial, *J'accuse*, is published on the front page of the Paris daily newspaper *L'Aurore*. Zola's impassioned essay polarizes France, driving it to the brink of civil war.

❧ The United States annexes the Hawaiian Islands and deposes Queen Liliuokalani in a brazen display of colonial effrontery. [Native Hawaiians are the last remaining indigenous group in the U.S. that has not been allowed to establish its own government].

❧ Turks in Heraklion, Greece, slaughter seven hundred Greeks and fifteen Englishmen.

❧ Bubonic plague erupts in China and India, killing an estimated three million people.

❧ Louisiana adopts a "grandfather clause" in a new constitution restricting black voting. Enacted by many southern states in the wake of Reconstruction, the statute allows white voters to circumvent literacy tests, poll taxes, and other tactics designed to disfranchise southern blacks. (More than a century later, the rhetoric of fear, racist pseudo-science, and social exclusion has reached an unprecedented level of stridency. There can be no doubt that every voter-suppression scheme, gerrymandering, and redistricting plot is calculated to send people of color back to the rear of the bus, to re-segregate schools and luncheonette counters, perhaps even to reinstate lynching as a means of sating the racist hankerings of America's heartland. At this writing, the state of Alabama, which requires a photo ID to vote, announced that it would be closing driver's license offices in thirty-one localities. The counties where the offices are to be shuttered are predominantly black and poor. These closures are yet another barrier to those seeking to exercise their right to dream through the ballot box. Citing a fictitious wave of voter fraud, most states, nearly all under Republican control, continue to enact laws making it more difficult for minorities to vote).

   ❧ The U.S. declares war on Spain, takes temporary control of Cuba and annexes Puerto Rico, Guam, and the Philippines.

   ❧ Seven thousand Jews are expelled from Kiev, Russia.

   ❧ A race riot erupts in Wilmington,

North Carolina, where a vigilante group of armed supremacists forcibly remove liberal black and white city leaders from office, burn buildings, and shoot scores of blacks.

ə Heroin is marketed as a cough "medicine."

ə Bubonic plague breaks out in San Francisco. Denying the presence of an epidemic, political leaders muzzle health officials. Anxious to prevent the loss of revenue from trade disrupted by quarantines, California Governor Henry Gage declares it a felony to mention the scourge. In the three years that follow, more than one hundred people die of "syphilitic septicemia," the official but fraudulent pseudonym of a disease that has nothing to do with syphilis or septicemia.

ə Japan ratifies a statute that discriminates against the Ainu people of Hokkaido. It scornfully describes them as aborigines "in need of assimilation." The decree is repealed one hundred years later.

ə Censured two years earlier, Anton Chekhov's play, *The Seagull,* opens to rave reviews at the Moscow Art Theatre. The drama conveys modern man's inability to find his "place." It exposes his subconscious yearning to be "elsewhere," and unmasks his painful sense of squandered dreams and denied hopes.

  ❧ *An Enemy of the People,* by Norwegian playwright Henrik Ibsen, is the story of how brave men can survive overwhelming odds. The play slams democracy for its complacent tolerance of undemocratic institutions. On one hand, leaders are at the mercy of a tyrannical majority; on the other the governed are afraid of risk and are too stupid, greedy, conformist, and spineless to rebel.

  ❧ Edvard Munch's painting, *The Scream,* starkly captures humankind's waking nightmare.

◆

In writing *A Dream Play,* which he called "my most beloved play, the child of my greatest pain," Strindberg said he attempted to…

> "…imitate the inconsequent yet transparently logical shape of dreams. Everything can happen; everything is possible and probable. Time and place do not exist; on an insignificant basis of reality, the imagination spins, weaving new patterns; a mixture of memories, experiences, free fancies, incongruities and improvisations. The characters split, double, multiply, evapo-

> *rate, condense, disperse and re-assemble. But
> one consciousness rules over them all, that of
> the dreamer; for him there are no secrets, no
> scruples, and no laws. He neither acquits nor
> condemns, but merely relates; and, just as a
> dream is more often painful than happy, so an
> undertone of melancholy and of pity for all
> mortal beings accompanies this flickering tale."*

Agnes, Strindberg's protagonist, is a daughter
of the Vedic god Indra. She descends to Earth
to bear witness to the evils perpetrated and
endured by mortals. She interacts with dozens
of characters, some of them having clearly a
symbolic status, including four gurus repre-
senting theology, philosophy, medicine, and
law. After experiencing all manner of human
indignities — poverty, materialism, class struggle, persecution, and the grinding routines of
family life — Agnes concludes that human beings are to be pitied. She returns to the cosmic
realm from whence she came and awakens
from the dream-like sequence of events, realiz-
ing that she too had become caught up in their
nightmares.

The "nightmare," I construed as the final
curtain came down, was the antithesis of a
universal dream whose features were at that

time unclear—more quixotic than pragmatic. The stirring counsel of an eminent Kabbalist would come to mind as I later mused over the play:

> *"In life, you don't get all the answers at once. First you must absorb and live with one simple truth. Then later you must find another truth, one that may seem to clash with and negate everything you previously knew. Then, from that confusion, emerges a higher truth: The inner light behind all you had learned before."*

I have since sought, found, and rejected other truths, and I have redefined the nightmare as an attempt by ideological storm troopers to impose their will and promote social, cultural, religious, and political standards that, instead of inspiring dreams, spawn unspeakable hallucinations.

SISYPHUS REDUX

Men are free only if they rule themselves. The suggestion that men can be both ruled and free is a lie perpetrated by advocates of governance-by-diktat. Sovereign people do not compromise their freedom or relinquish their dreams. However, given to foolishness, cowardice, gullibility, and sloth, often seduced by simplistic ideas, deceptive speechifying, and false hopes, some people will unwittingly surrender their birthright of life, liberty and the pursuit of happiness to individuals and institutions whose strategy is to alter reality and obliterate millennial dreams in favor of a select few who believe that only they are entitled to live and be happy.

To be governed [ruled] is to be stalked, scrutinized, spied on, dictated to, controlled, restrained, indoctrinated, sermonized, reprimanded and bullied by swaggering automatons who have no couth, wisdom, or virtue. To be ruled [monitored] is to have every gesture scrutinized, every word dissected, every transaction noted, recorded, tallied, graded, measured, taxed, licensed, denied, approved, sanctioned, rebuked, banned, converted, and ultimately altered to suit the aims and welfare of the governing elite. Should some future Machiavellian science permit, will unlicensed or seditious dreamers be the targets of witch-hunts? Can our musings be intercepted and censored? Will the neurons in our brain be re-wired to turn incommodious men into servile conformists? All else failing, will they be liquidated?

Isn't the clash of dreams the real cause of humankind's afflictions?

In another work where I explore the consequences of mind control and robotizing in a society that abhors free thought, reviles erudition, mocks intellect and dreads the truth, in short a world where morality is little more than a distillate of codified groupthink, I ask:

> *"Will there soon be a way to retrieve and deci-pher the brain's most quirky concepts? Will ethicists struggle with a new conundrum – dreamers being spied upon by some future thought police? How long before eccentric nightmares or heretical concepts, whether seized in one's sleep or evoked in a wakeful state, are intercepted and wayward dreamers are reprogrammed or permanently silenced? After all, aren't latter-day auto-da-fés targeting freethinkers, mavericks and dissenters who must be neutralized or muzzled if special inter-ests are to maintain their imperial grip on mankind?*[2]

To be free implies the existence of mecha-nisms that empower men to protect their physical freedom without surrendering their dreams. One such device, so far inaccessible in "civilized" societies, is the license to defend against the evils of greed and protect from the rivalries that promote ownership, turn com-petitiveness into a revered blood sport, and glorify the idolatrous worship of power and money.

---

[2] *One Last Dream* (© 2012).

Since antiquity, cultivation of the earth has nurtured avarice and prompted the fencing of lands that had no legitimate or entitled holder but through thievery and the force of arms, thus leading to the rise of the principle of "property." Once "landlords" began to claim ownership of grounds seized illicitly, the dissimilarity between the landed and the landless led to a dismal inequality of fortunes. Wealth (and the complicity of those who stood to profit by coddling the rich) empowered some men to enslave other men and to argue on strictly monetary grounds that, being profitable, serfdom is therefore justifiable.

This perspective has since made respectable the argument that commercial interests supersede the welfare of individuals — those whose ceaseless and profitless exertions contribute to the enrichment of the wealthy. Seen in that light, it is no hyperbole to assert that having to work for someone else at obscenely low wages, while pushing a rock up a hill only to see it tumble back down, is a form of slavery, and that, by extension, ownership is theft.

Indeed, the very idea of custody, of proprietorship, continues to inflame passions and lead to discord, quarrels, sometimes even war, and, lo and behold, to strident calls for the curtailment of civil liberties. It is the rich who clamor the loudest for "law and order;" for while unrest and violence impact everyone, it is worse for the moneyed elite because their possessions are at risk. Having gotten rich the old-fashioned way—by stealing—they will stop at nothing to protect their assets and acquire more wealth.

The business of "governing" has been gradually surrendered to a class of snollygosters, shysters and sycophants keen on wielding power and getting rich, not dedicated to the welfare of the society they are sworn to serve and protect, less yet to the ideals that such society professes to champion. Claiming "personhood," corporations are chipping away at a once commanding and now frittering middle class, and creating a neo-feudal system that exacts tireless subjection and enforced obedience from the growing tide of serfs that uninhibited capitalism keeps spawning. As the number of plutocrats grows, so will poverty, oppression, enslavement and discontent among the working class. No generation of robber barons lives more openly by force, fraud and sophistry than the tycoons of our time. No species is more on the brink of extinction than the middle class.

A MALIGNANT HYDRA

Capitalism is not interested in improving people's lives, less yet in underwriting their dreams or shielding them from the colossal immorality of the free market, from the inequities with which it is fraught, or from the scams to which it resorts in order to prevail. It is a hard-hearted, self-replicating, and malignant hydra whose sole purpose is to create more capital.

Exploitation is the cornerstone of capitalism. To thrive, capitalism depends on an awkward partnership between uneven but mutually dependent coconspirators. They include, at the very top, the direct beneficiaries of capital: entrepreneurs, owners, and financiers who have more wealth than they know what to do with but who, for the thrill of it, want to make *more* money; politicians who put themselves at the service of capital; legislators who craft the laws dictated to them by special interests; and bankers who favor the rich and empower those who rule by profiting from the system. At the bottom rung of a very tall ladder stands the working class, an involuntary accomplice and the actual producer of a wealth it can never hope to acquire because of larcenous fiscal policies, predatory taxation, hidden levies, legal loopholes and a perpetually rising cost of living kept artificially high to favor the seller to the detriment of the consumer. What the system chews and spits out are those who have already been rejected because they are essentially useless, if not detrimental to a society that reveres entrepreneurship, idolizes youth, beauty and brawn—the homely and the homeless, the jobless and the unskilled, the old and the sick, undocumented immigrants, and asylum seekers, in short, the detritus who do not die fast enough, that annoying sub-caste of poor, unserviceable trespassers who disturb public order simply because they exist.

Governments are not erected for the benefit of the governed. They would collapse if they did. Political authority looks at human society as consisting of disparate herds of sheep, each in need of a shepherd, some inevitably less benevolent than others, who control the flock the better to devour its members. The most ingenious shepherds can never be powerful enough to control the whole herd unless they turn might into right, and coerced subservience into mandated obligation. Thus, force cannot foster morality. Men yield to force out of necessity, fear, or prudence, not free will. Only when they are free to flout the constrictions that imperil or extinguish their dreams, can they legitimize their insubordination.

Far from protecting their subjects (except in a lucky few Socialist countries), governments, like epiphytes, graft themselves onto them for sustenance and survival. Citizens are led to believe that their leaders provide civil tranquility. But how does that benefit them when greed and wars of ideological domination abroad cause more desolation and discontent at home?

◆

A government is legitimate only if its citizens are free to accept or reject the strictures it imposes and the phony dreams it peddles. To surrender one's dreams is to renounce one's humanity, to strip life of all moral significance; it is contrary to human nature. So long as some amass colossal fortunes while others can't find work and mothers can't feed their children and big pharmaceutical companies gouge the people with sky-high drug prices and conscripts are force-marched to wars not of their choosing, dreamers will be forced to choose between power and violence bereft of love and love bereft of power. The strength of dreamers is effective only if it is focused; it weakens and is squandered when it is dispersed. Dreamers must do what others cannot do in their stead. They must fight without respite against dogmatism and idolatry. Moral indignation leads to revolution more often than poverty or hunger. It took the upheavals of humanity, the tribal instinct of cannibalism, racism and nationalism for 21st century societies to reconnect consciously to an ancient ideal — the universality of moral man.

The wider the distance between ruler and the people, the greater is the opportunity for injustice. It is to the advantage of rulers that the flock shall be weak, wretched and never able to resist. Fortunately, the body politic, much like the human organism, begins to decay as soon as it is born. It bears within itself the seed of its own demise.[3] It is when it shows signs of fatigue, asymmetry, discord and intellectual decrepitude that dreamers can rise, say, NO, and turn dreams into action. As Leon Trotsky wrote,

> *"As long as human labor power, and, consequently, life itself, remain articles of sale and purchase, of exploitation and robbery, the principle of the 'sacredness of human life' remains a shameful lie, uttered with the object of keeping the oppressed slaves in their chains."*

◆

With economic inequality at its highest level in nearly a century and public debate rising over whether the government should react by levying higher taxes on the wealthy, an article published in December 2015 in *The New York Times*, alleges that plutocrats quietly manipulate tax policy in their favor and that the wealthiest Americans have financed an arcane

---

[3] *Will Cuppy, The Rise and Fall of Practically Everybody.*

and shockingly effective apparatus for hiding their fortunes and sheltering them from scrutiny.

The report further asserts that operating largely out of public view—in tax court, through obscure legislative loopholes, and in private negotiations with the Internal Revenue Service—the rich use their power to steadily whittle away at the government's ability to tax them. The result has been the creation of a secretive and elitist tax system catering to a select few Americans.

In America, justice is a commodity accessible only to those who can pay for it.

♦

The rich are destroying the world's economic structure and human culture. They hold powers and enjoy privileges they refuse to relinquish. They will resort to every abomination, including war, to protect them.

Perhaps only a revolution can strip them of their deadly arsenal.

THE STUFF THAT

NIGHTMARES ARE MADE OF

Devoid of empathy and altruism as its sole mission, science does not, will not save ailing societies, or cure those suffocating under a surfeit of technological innovations. Progress is a tempting illusion. What appears to be "advancement" is in reality a perpetual status quo swarming with intentionally obsolescent novelties that do nothing to refine the mind or ennoble the spirit. We ventured out of caves and traded nomadism for a life of hunting, gathering, and, later farming. We then surrendered to a troglodytic existence in densely populated concrete and steel beehives girded by train depots, crisscrossed by congested thoroughfares, surrounded by chemical and sewage treatment plants, refineries, and smoke-belching factories. In our haste to seek strength and safety in numbers, we overlooked one basic human idiosyncrasy: When herded together and compelled to be sociable — meaning unconditional surrender to arbitrary covenants — we become unsociable.

Eventually, we challenged and conquered gravity, erected orbital space stations, carved our footsteps on the Moon, landed robotic craft on Mars, and sent probes on scouting errands to the farthest reaches of the inky void. We now communicate with the aid of irritating gadgets that have transformed us into petty-minded, monosyllabic chatterboxes, and reduced meaningful dialogue to trivial babble. "Smart" phones are turning people into jabbering idiots. Computer games, which awaken the dormant but by no means defunct reptilian brain, lure impressionable minds and immerse them in worlds of titillating virtual violence.

Testosterone-driven creatures promised papal indulgences for our sins, we embarked on Church-sanctioned centuries-long military campaigns — the Crusades — in which thousands of Jews, Muslims and Albigenses were slaughtered. Designed to combat "heresy" and augment the Vatican's fortunes, the "Holy" Inquisition tortured and exterminated two hundred thousand men, women and children. We later took time to wage wars to end all wars and wars of liberation during which we pulverized Coventry and Dresden, Le Havre and Rotterdam, Nagasaki and Hiroshima; wars of religion, fratricide and genocide; wars of occupation and economic colonization; illegal, unwinnable and ruinous wars premised on exceptionalism and a diseased brand of patriotism, and scripted to achieve hegemonic dominance (Iraq, Afghanistan); wars of reprisal (Korea, Vietnam); wars of arrogance and spite (Grenada, Panama). There will be other wars.

Yes, we begat Socrates and Shakespeare, Leonardo and Locke, Mozart and Michelangelo, Empedocles and Einstein ... and spawned Attila and Hitler and Stalin and Mao and Pol Pot and Idi Amin and Ceausescu and Saddam and Kim Il Sung and Pinochet and Gaddafi and.... Deep down, we are unenlightened beings on whom science and technology, creature comforts, and unprecedented abundance are foisting moral ruin. The evolution of modern civilization has not made man happier or more virtuous. He can find happiness only in a state of nature and unhindered freedom. Everything else is the *illusion* of happiness. We feign serenity but we are consumed with worry. We laugh in order not to cry. Hope is the panacea for all that threatens us, pains us, offends us; hope is our antidote against reality. Whereas virtue is the gift of simple unassimilated societies where people can live unassuming and frugal lives untainted by modernity and in voluntary isolation from its debasing influence of modernity. Sophisticated societies corrupt men; the greater the sophistication, the more noxious the sophistry, the viler the corruption.

Meanwhile, as politicians give in to the demands of plutocratic elites, tell lies to justify war, and use hired thugs to stir hatred and provoke violence in other people's backyards, we learn of the obscenities that uncontrolled use of fossil fuels are wreaking upon our tired planet. By the end of this century, large swatches of the Persian Gulf will be overwhelmed by waves of heat and humidity so severe as to threaten human life. The poles are melting; glaciers are cracking, splitting apart and dissolving. As a result, oceans are rising.

According to a World Bank report, rising sea levels from unchecked carbon emissions could drive more than one hundred million people into extreme poverty and submerge the homes of over half a billion.

Climate-related "shocks," the report affirms, are already impeding efforts to reduce poverty, particularly through crop losses, food price shocks, and other impacts on agriculture, which is the main source of income for most poor families. Climate change also increases the risk of waterborne diseases, with a warming of 2°C to 3°C likely to put an extra one hundred and fifty million people at risk for malaria and other insect-transmitted diseases. The report also notes that ending poverty and fighting climate change cannot be done in isolation.

Teeming with harmful substances such as oil, plastics, industrial and agricultural waste, and toxic chemicals, seas are acidifying and imperiling marine life. Reefs are dying. Rivers are contaminated. Lakes are turning into fetid cesspools. Pollution and fires decimate timberlands. Cyclones and torrential rains grow in intensity and frequency. Heat waves and desertification keep spreading across the globe. Parched, grasslands shrivel under an implacable sun. Nations are disintegrating. Tribal groups are disappearing and, with them, the languages they spoke, the arts and crafts, the music, dances, values and oral traditions that gave them their unique identity. Five thousand languages and dialects are still being spoken around the world; twenty-five vanish every year. By the end of this century, half of them will be dead. Life—human, animal and vegetal—faces extinction and with it, countless dreams.

◆

The myth, *"all men are created equal,"* is born of delusional reasoning. If that were true, all men would be rich (or poor); smart (or stupid); healthy (or sick); talented (or inept); resourceful (or unimaginative); virtuous (or wicked); fated to lead other men (or be enslaved by them). But even the strongest man cannot be master unless he transfers or relinquishes some of his authority to accomplices whose allegiance—sweetened by favors, perks and back-room pacts—shield him from dethronement and dispossession. The best that can be said is that, accidents of birth notwithstanding, not all men have access to the same opportunities. Without a fight, we are all destined to inherit life's burdens and none of its blessings. Without the dreams, we must endure the undifferentiating oddness of existence or succumb to the fiends impaled at our throats.

Remember sweet, tragic Anne Frank. She believed in man's innate goodness and dreamed of a world where love conquers all. She was wrong and was martyred at the altar of her own naiveté. If she'd been right, she and some fifteen million innocent souls — Jews, Slavs, Gypsies, Armenians, homosexuals—would not have been force-marched and herded in cattle cars and consigned to Hitler's extermination camps. Having survived the Holocaust, and outlived it, I believe it is in mankind's genetic makeup to produce monsters. We cannot afford to presume that other monsters are not, at this very moment, gestating in their mothers' wombs.

There will be other genocides. The brutality that animates them is so horrific that we give them prosaic names: nation building; humanitarian peace efforts; police action; limited engagement; neutralization; counterinsurgency operation; surgical strike; regime change; and the most sinister of all — democratization.

◆

"When human statecraft attaches a chain to the feet of a free man, whom it makes a slave in contempt of nature and citizenship, eternal justice rivets the other end about the tyrant's neck."

So declared Louis Antoine de St. Just (1767-1794), one of the architects of the French Revolution, a long-simmering explosive event that would purge France, for the first time in its history, from the yoke of feudalism, absolute monarchy and religious despotism.

Dubbed the "angel of death," so ferocious was his commitment to an insurrection born of centuries of royal mismanagement, corruption, oppression and exploitation by all-powerful aristocratic and ecclesiastical elites, St. Just argued that man is a social animal and that in nature there is no need for contracts, legislation, or acts of force. Of course, there's so very little nature left that men are forced into ever-narrowing and increasingly congested enclaves, that they must substitute the natural bonds of free people with artificial conventions. Regrettably, these conventions empower small cliques to assume control over the masses, leading to corruption, inequality and injustice. The weak and the voiceless must be immolated so that the strong may continue to rule.

While society's first law is to safeguard the armatures that protect it, man's first law is to ensure his sovereignty and reaffirm his personhood in a world that sacrifices individuals for the good of the group. Only then can he become his own master and defend against individuals, corporate entities, and practices that do him harm, that deny him the right to dream, and that stimulate the proliferation of subversive mindsets: Stock market manipulators; rising income inequality; courts that consistently rule in favor of the rich and powerful; hostile takeovers; xenophobic politicians; mega churches; lobbyists; hate groups; states' rights advocates; blinkered office-holders; war-mongering generals; gun merchants; privately-owned and –run correctional institutions; for-profit healthcare; price-gouging pharmaceutical companies; chemical manufacturers; genetically-modified food producers; insurance companies; dishonest lawyers, sadistic cops, to name a few. These enemies of truth, these Orwellian dream-busters will never come to their senses.

Unless.

THE TOXIC NORMALCY OF CORRUPTION

Franklin Delano Roosevelt said, "Government by organized money is as dangerous as government by organized mob." Sensing that foreign policy is strictly about power and narrow interests [whereas a growing right-wing fringe deems values and morals to be for the feeble-minded] President *"I like Ike"* Dwight D. Eisenhower warned against the evils of the military-industrial complex and the lure of armed entanglements. Economists and social scientists cautioned against the very excesses that, six decades later, would turn the U.S. into a putative gangdom dedicated to enriching a privileged few by emasculating a once thriving middle class and further impoverishing the poor. If a system is built on power but lacks legitimacy, behaviorists added, it will destroy itself. If it asserts moral truths but lacks the power to enforce them, it will unravel. Their counsel fell on deaf ears. What we now have is government of the rich, by the rich and for the rich. A corruptible mob of vultures waits to feed on the carcasses of those who do not survive its predacious ways.

◆

Corruptibility is the mother of all vices. Without it we'd be living in a fiction-like world of virtue, magnanimity and justice. It is as powerful an impulse as the reproductive urge or the survival instinct. Because we're human, we're all susceptible to its siren song. Self-delusion and the perversion of reality as a hedge against the sobering effect of reason are its commonest forms.

Also predisposed toward corruptibility are those whose conduct can be manipulated. Pretending to be what our parents, teachers, spiritual leaders, employers and the tax collector expect of us can result in small rewards or, at the very least, it can protect us from censure or chastisement. And then there are those who can be corrupted by money and will do any-thing for it — lie, cheat, betray, torture, and even kill — particularly in the poorest countries but by no means limited to them. Corruption is the bedrock in which business and govern-ance are anchored. It's become a habitual, rit-ualized, institutionalized reflex. It's part of the social fabric. People have become so inured to it that they no longer recognize it for what it really is: the process of putrefaction by which nations decompose and eventually collapse.

There is a direct correlation between how people are empowered in their societies and their leaders' propensity to circumvent basic covenants, to prevaricate, to be suborned and to engage in the wholesale sellout of their citi-zens. Where people have an unimpeded voice in their own affairs, and where a lively civil culture thrives, those in authority have a harder time evading public scrutiny, harder yet in dodging public censure.

In contrast, in a growing number of cryp-to-autocratic nations where wealth and politi-cal might are concentrated in small, affluent, all-powerful circles, people have a nominal voice but no clout, especially where their vital interests—life, liberty and the pursuit of happiness—are curtailed and further weakened by poverty, endemic violence and the appalling indifference and incompetence of their leaders. John Q. Public just doesn't count; he's expendable. Those who protest are either ignored, their grievances lost in the murky corridors of bureaucracy, or they risk surveillance harassment, persecution, incarceration, and even death.

"We've been reduced to turning our heads and looking the other way," said a Central American appellate court judge on condition of anonymity. "We overlook corruption because doing otherwise would have grave consequences. To identify oneself as a paladin is to stand out. Paladins don't die of old age."

Other dynamics prevent people from listening to their conscience. One of them is the stupefying realization that elected officials, given their own venality and the tangled intrigues in which they engage, sometimes in cahoots with criminal elements, are so inextricably ensnared in shady activities that they couldn't fix the problems they created even if they tried. This is especially true of so-called "developing countries," a euphemism for hopelessly stagnant, backward, or failed states.

Sleaze comes in two flavors: Corruption of opportunism and corruption of necessity. The former exists since the Earth cooled. It will thrive wherever cunning humans congregate. The latter occurs when, reduced to their primal state, and unable to survive by any other means, otherwise decent human beings misbehave. This syncretism is not coincidental. The more impoverished a nation becomes when capital is held in fewer hands, the greater the temptation and opportunity to deceive and defraud.

Corruption does not occur in a vacuum. It's a system of values and behaviors that entails collusion between consenting entities: The corrupted and the corruptor.

♦

Just as a shipbuilder's sacred obligation is to ensure a vessel's seaworthiness, so must a government determine, on its own free will (if it is honest), or by populist-mandated plebiscites, whether the laws it enacts are beneficial or prejudicial to *all* its citizens. Mindful that the rich, who consider egalitarianism and justice harmful to their interests, will by instinct or inclination prevent it from governing fairly, an honest government would have to seek another vision of society, an alternative to a socio-economic system that tolerates so much poverty, so many broken dreams to fester in the midst of plenty. This model of governance presumes that an "honest government" is not just an offensive oxymoron.

Left to their own devices men will be led by their passions, or the follies of others, to perdition. Some will lose the capacity to dream. Others will forfeit their right to envisage a brighter reality because they fear the wrath of those who, by promoting evil virtues — selfishness, objectivism, capital accumulation, cronyism, wage slavery, and corporate welfare — have the power to extinguish their dreams.

The crises now facing millions of desperate dreamers seeking freedom and redemption have carved deep fissures that threaten to tear the dreams to shreds. They desperately need to be saved from their tormentors. Some — the meek, the irresolute, the destitute, the terrified — may have to be *compelled* to be free so they can more forcefully strike back. Time has come to arm the powerless, to infuriate and disarm the powerful.

In the strict sense of the word, there has never been a true democracy, and there will never be until the greater number governs the smaller one. The shame of it all is that when people don't react against bad governance (out of sloth, fear, indifference, stupidity — mostly stupidity) politicians exploit the situation. The problem is that those who are well off aren't interested in change and those who are not well off don't have the power to effect change. This condition attracts fascism, a system that pretends to foster change while avoiding it — or worse.

THE MAGNIFICENT MARQUIS

I have no idols, alive or dead. Other than my late father, an iron-willed and incorruptible man, I admire few people, in or out of the limelight. It takes an exceptional blend of creative genius, integrity, and compassion to earn a person my esteem, let alone the praise of posterity. Intellect, altruism, and temerity in the face of ignorance, superstition, and hatred are virtues I find most inspiring. Descartes, Galileo, Father Damien, Albert Schweitzer, Henry David Thoreau, Mahatma Gandhi, Martin Luther King, best represent these ideals. I also have a fondness for infidels, humanists and firebrands: Giordano Bruno, Italian philosopher, mathematician and poet (imprisoned for seven years in a medieval dungeon then burned at the stake in 1600 for "holding opinions contrary to the Catholic faith and speaking against it and its ministers"); François-Noël Babeuf, French radical, political agitator and journalist guillotined in 1797. He famously said, "Society must be made to operate in such a way as to eradicate once and for all the cravings of men to become richer, or wiser, or more powerful than others;" Pierre-Joseph Proudhon, French polemicist, journalist and self-described anarchist who defined ownership as "theft;" Jacques Roux, a radical Roman Catholic priest who took an active role in the politics of the French Revolution and became a leader of the far-left. Roux skillfully expounded the ideals of popular democracy and classless society to crowds of Parisian low-wage earners and shopkeepers, radicalizing them into an active revolutionary force; William Lloyd Garrison, 19th century American abolitionist, journalist, suffragist, and social reformer; Emma Goldman (memorable anarchist who rejected orthodoxy and fundamentalist thinking); and Robert Ingersoll (nicknamed "The Great Agnostic,") a lawyer,

American Civil War veteran, political leader, and orator during the Golden Age of Free Thought.

For upholding the noblest traditions and objectives of journalism summarized in the Chapultepec Declaration—

> *"...A free society can thrive only through free expression and the exchange of ideas, the search for and the dissemination of information, the ability to investigate and question, to propound and react, to agree and disagree, to converse and confront, to publish and broadcast.... Only through open discussion and unfettered information will it be possible to find answers to the great collective problems, to reach consensus, to have development benefit all sectors, to practice social justice and to advance the quest for equality.... Without freedom there can be no true order, stability, or justice. And without freedom of expression there can be no freedom."* —

I add, without a trace of hesitation, my favorite whistleblowers: Bradley Manning (now serving a 35-year prison sentence under the Espionage Act), and Julian Assange and Edward Snowden, both facing stiff prison sentences (if caught and brought to justice) both destined to suffer the eternal scorn of an ungrateful nation. Another proof that no good deed goes unpunished. Not far behind stand Ralph Nader, mocked scorned and trivialized, for reminding us that we are unsafe at any speed; Dr. Kevorkian, for daring to suggest that we are entitled to die with dignity; Mary Schiavo, a tireless crusader for flight safety who exposed fraud, corruption, waste, mismanagement, and criminal negligence in the aviation industry and the FAA; Karen Silkwood, who fought for worker safety at the chemical plant where she worked; and Erin Brokovitch, who continues to help people who have suffered because of environmental contamination, defective medical devices, and tainted or ineffective pharmaceuticals.

I can't say when or how this reverence for moral fiber, pluck, and chutzpah began but, for as long as I can remember, I've been heaping praise on less than perfect men who, while navigating the dark, shark-infested waters of ignorance, superstition and fear, manage to alter their nation's character and destiny. Inevitably, when I think of these individuals I also imagine how hopelessly stalled societies would benefit from their ideas, skills, and strength of character, were they still alive to-day.

One such almost mythical character, little known outside the Iberian Peninsula, is the controversial 18th century go-getter, Sebastiáo José de Carvalho e Mello, better known of the Marquis of Pombal. Virtual leader of the king-dom of Portugal at a time of turmoil and sec-tarian bloodshed, he is considered by the Por-tuguese as their greatest statesman and a champion of their dreams and aspirations.

Pombal's crowning achievement was the disbandment of the Inquisition in Portugal and Spain, and the introduction of administra-tive, educational, economic and ecclesiastical reforms inspired by "Reason" — a heretical concept the almighty Church despised and feared. He was instrumental in advancing secularism and promoting a free press at a time when the "Holy" Inquisition barbecued people for entertaining inconvenient dreams (or for having had Jewish or Muslim ancestry). Pombal, who lived for a time in Vienna and London, the latter being a major center of the Enlightenment, believed that the Jesuits, with their grip on science and education, hindered an independent Portuguese-style democratic *iluminismo*. Given that Jesuits were the chief inquisitors in Portugal, Pombal's efforts against them greatly weakened and eventually loosened their grip in Europe and the colonies.

Pombal is remembered for his swift and competent leadership in the aftermath of the devastating 1755 earthquake that leveled Lisbon and killed one hundred thousand people. He implemented sweeping economic policies to regulate commercial activity and standardize manufacturing quality control. His greatest reforms were economic and financial, with the creation of several companies and guilds. He ruled with a heavy hand that favored the working class and imposed the strict equality of law upon all citizens. These reforms earned him enemies among aristocrats and members of the clergy who feared him, calling him a social upstart, a heretic and an agitator.

In 1759 he expelled the Jesuits who had a stranglehold on education. He instituted a secular, public primary and secondary school system, introduced vocational training, created hundreds of new teaching posts, added departments of mathematics and natural sciences to the University of Coimbra, and introduced new taxes to fund these groundbreaking innovations. Even the Vatican reluctantly admits that:

"In the political sphere [Pombal's] *administration was marked by boldness of conception and tenacity of purpose. He leveled all classes, imposed absolute obedience to the law, which was largely decided by himself because the tribunals had long ceased to function, and he transformed the Inquisition into an insignificant and largely impotent department of the state."*

The Marquis' most notable legislative victories include the abolition of Indian slavery and the odious distinction between Christians and Jewish [forced] converts to Christianity.

Fear of enlightenment during the Inquisition, as it persists today in many parts of the world, was such that censorship, by intimidation, persecution and indifference to human suffering, became the main preoccupation of the ruling classes. Then and now, scholars saw the curtailment of knowledge and free thought, and the concentration of wealth in a handful of dynastic families, as resulting in the growing intellectual decrepitude of society. A form of inquisition still festers — the immutable socio-economic and cultural vice-like grip on the masses by all-powerful elites and self-styled arbiters of morality.

Some readers will call the foregoing three-century rearward leap in time a trivial pursuit, or its intimations inapplicable to the present. I disagree. The past has always been prologue and an immovable past, like an immovable present, is a sure recipe for disaster. Added to brute fact, trivia can be invaluable. It puts meat on the bone of history. It also warns hooligans and profiteers that posterity is watching and is poised to strike back.

NEW DREAMS FOR OLD

History is full of dreamers who sought to create what they imagined to be a perfect world — generally without the world's consent and more often than not to its detriment. Moses dreamed up a set of directives that are stubbornly ignored. Infused with messianic fervor and self-predestination, Jesus attempted to spread Judaism among Gentiles. His disciples misrepresented his message and anti-Semitism was born. Caesar's *Pax Romana* was extorted by brute force and the Republic fell. The prophet Muhammad branded the souls of his converts with an austere, warlike simulation of the Judeo-Christian pipedream. Crusaders — hoodlums, religious terrorists and soldiers of fortune — massacred Jews and Muslims in a quest to "reclaim" the "Holy Land" for Christianity, a religion that did not gain official status until 325 years after the death of Jesus. Led by the Church and financed by kings, the Inquisition sent thousands of "heretics" to the stake after systematically robbing them of their possessions.

Brandishing a sword in one hand, wielding the Cross in the other, the Conquista, during which the crusader's fanaticism and the inquisitor's ferocity reached their apogee, left a trail of blood that stretched from Mexico to Patagonia. Grandiose ambitions, ill-fated coalitions, and empire-building wars put an end to Napoleon's vision of a unified Europe. Karl Marx called for the equal distribution of goods produced collectively. Well-to-do and contemptuous of the proletariat, Marx forgot that greed gets in the way of altruism, that ideals are devoured by ideology. So Stalin and Mao hijacked Marx's grand delusion and turned it into a nightmare that nearly extinguished mankind's last hope for redemption. Hell-bent on creating a robotized master race, Hitler shattered millions of dreams and tarnished

Germany's image. They all invaded our space, aiming to impose their standards of reality on a world that breeds with reckless abandon and can barely feed itself.

♦

Utopians never do evil, or lapse into stupidity, so readily and fulsomely as when driven by conviction. Take the proposed creation of "model societies," idyllic visions of a world free of crime, garbage, lung-searing pollution, contaminated drinking water and riotous traffic, magnificent conurbations cleansed of embarrassing "pariahs" — the destitute, the homeless, the delinquents — and overseen by righteous, magnanimous futurists–turned–politicians whose only objective is to improve the lives of their fellow dreamers ... by consigning them to an untested, bizarre and alien domain of Utopian dimensions.

In the abstract, properly inspired and wisely processed, model societies can be a paradigm for human self-renewal. In the hands of buccaneers, opportunity turns into opportunism, opportunism into corruption and criminality. Soon, the Utopian dream becomes a dystopian nightmare.

Philosopher Karl Popper, who cautioned that intolerance should not be tolerated, "for if tolerance allowed bigotry to succeed, tolerance would be imperiled," warned that Utopia tends toward despotism. Nobel Prize winning writer, Mario Vargas Llosa added that the idea of a perfect society is the trademark of monsters: "When you want paradise you first generate extraordinary idealism. You then produce hell." Llosa was referring to the tyranny of inflexible dogmas — ultra-nationalism and religion's despotism and fanciful promise of an afterlife. But he was also guarding against the notion that otherwise noble reveries can materialize without risk or counter-intuitive consequences.

Model societies? In a world that cannot feed the poor, a world where a small moneyed elite reigns supreme over growing throngs crippled by penury and hopelessness? A world so chaotic and vulnerable that politicians ad-lib policies, shun basic responsibilities and govern without a long-term blueprint for the future? Will these Nirvanas be cemented with love and generosity, wisdom and enlightenment; or will the decaying dreams of broken men be dumped in the garbage pit of history? Will they rise far from the blight, bedlam and putrefaction of man's insatiable greed and triumph over the ruins of his unfulfilled expectations?

Utopia is Greek word. It means "no place;" *"nowhere."* It exists only in the minds of mystics and charlatans. Model societies? Models of what? Are they, like Thomas More's fantastical template, ideological traps designed to ensnare the naïve and compliant while earning land developers and real-estate manipulators huge fortunes?

Wouldn't a model *dream* that benefits everyone be immensely more useful? A dream in which the rich stop stealing, stop deceiving, stop corrupting elected officials, stop gouging the public, stop dodging taxes, stop poisoning the planet, and start heeding the wishes of this and future generations?

WHEN THE RICH PLAY, THE POOR PAY

Parallel universes (or alternate realities in which the laws of physics are not only dissimilar but in conflict) is the stuff of science fiction and quantum mechanics. Brought down to Earth, the concept takes on sinister dimensions.

Coexisting side-by-side in states of reciprocal insensitivity, one spurred by greed, the other the victims of prolonged penury, are the filthy rich and people on the verge of destitution. This is the face of modern feudalism. Not known for their altruism or high moral values, corporations—as the number of malnourished and homeless Americans keeps rising — continue to peddle complex securities (synthetic collateralized debt obligations) to the tune of $110 billion then bet against them and laugh all the way... to the bank.

On one side is the funfair of the hyper-rich, who indulge in high-risk stunts for the thrill of it. Abutting it is the dirt back lot of the super poor. As financial institutions create billions of dollars worth of disastrously performing mortgage-linked debt instruments and wager against the clients who purchased them, more and more Americans are sinking into poverty. What little food they can scrape to keep the heart pumping is far less than enough to turn into muscle. Mounting an offensive against their moneyed tormentors is an empty wish.

Once upon a time, there was an American Dream: prosperity for all. Now, fifty million Americans go hungry, including five million seniors and half a million children. Lines at soup kitchens and food stamp offices are getting longer. Although the mainstream media have generally kept mum about these statistics, they are real. They come from the U.S. Department of Agriculture, which has published them yearly since 1995. The figures do not take into account jobless rates, which, at this writing, are said to have been brought down to statistically more acceptable levels, but which persist, especially among those whose unemployment benefits ran out and who no longer bother to look for inexistent work. Indeed, among the victims of hunger, the USDA also notes the prevalence of the working poor, people who live at or below the poverty level while earning subsistence wages. Scandalously, people who work one hour a week are considered fully employed!

◆

Language is a wondrous and mighty tool used to define, distort or conceal the truth. Power over words means power over ideas, and power over ideas translates into power over people. Governments exert considerable influence on our thoughts in the way they wield power through language. One method carried to diabolical limits is "doublespeak," an ornate and allegorical idiom fashioned to disguise the actual meaning of things, and usually employed by politicians, the military and commerce to bamboozle, hoodwink and swindle the credulous, the ignorant and the uninformed.

Some of the figurative lingo coined by do-gooders — terms such as "animal companions" for pets, "challenged" for handicapped, "wardrobe malfunction" for a runaway nipple or an unzipped fly, and "consolidation" or "downsizing" for merciless firings — evokes smiles, compassion, amusement or scorn. Grammar calls these dialectical deceptions "euphemisms." In his visionary novel, *1984,* George Orwell dubbed them "newspeak" and "doublethink," fashionable composite nouns...

> "...deliberately constructed for political purposes: words which not only have a political implication, but are intended to impose a desirable mental attitude upon those using them."

Take the U.S. Army's recruitment slogan, *"Be an Army of One."* This moronic oxymoron surely appeals to the gung-ho "let's-kill-the-gooks-and-ragheads" jingoes, but the reality of soldiering includes unquestioned obedience to authority and unavoidable risks that include mutilation and disfigurement, insanity, and death. Doublespeak is most reminiscent of Orwell's "newspeak" when it is articulated by government agencies to cover up some mortifying peccadillo or ignominy. They might reluctantly be forced to address topics that have negative connotations for large segments of the public. To avoid a backlash of bad publicity, they will replace a term with a new one that most people will fail to recognize as signifying the same thing. Thus, "area denial munitions" means land mines. "Rendition" stands for the illegal kidnapping of suspects who are then handed over to the authorities of another nation for grilling.

"Enhanced interrogation techniques" is doublespeak for torture. "Operational exhaustion" stands for shellshock. "Collateral damage" whitewashes the "accidental" slaughter of civilians. "Suspected terrorist hideout" refers to any home destroyed by U.S. troops. "Asymmetrical warfare" describes imaginative combat tactics used by the "bad guys" before the "good guys" had a chance to think of it.... "Self-injurious behavior incident" alludes to attempted suicide. Decoded, "USA Patriot Act" translates into "Uniting and Strengthening America by Providing Appropriate Tools Required to Intercept and Obstruct Terrorist Acts"—a decree rammed through without debate or national referendum, despite the fact that it deals a devastating blow to civil liberties while granting the government unlimited powers and virtually no oversight. The USA Patriot Act was swiftly reinforced with a program dubbed "Total Information Awareness" which, once stripped of its pseudo-techno veneer, means, "spying on the citizenry without probable cause." Whereas economic terrorism, a form of passive violence used by rich countries to give poor ones a hiding, is referred to as an "embargo." Democracy, a commodity America is eager to export, sometimes by force of arms, but is loath to cultivate at home, enables this newfangled inquisition.

◆

If the above mumbo-jumbo were not enough to set off a collective heave of revulsion, a key government report on malnourishment eliminated the word "hunger" to describe a chronic condition affecting sixteen percent of American households. People without enough money to buy food, families in which parents skip meals so children can eat, and seniors who must choose between dinner and life-saving drugs are now grotesquely categorized as having "very low food security."

This masquerade is based on hair-splitting

recommendations from "scholars" who can't decide whether people are hungry or merely have "limited access to food." Such skewed reasoning suggests that the fifty million people who rely on food stamps, soup kitchens and other charities for their daily sustenance are not necessarily hungry. They just don't know where their next meal is coming from. "Food insecurity" is an obscene term calculated to ease the collective conscience while artfully underplaying what amounts to a national tragedy and a disgrace.

Inflated and skyrocketing drug prices are killing people. The U.S. pharmaceutical industry is forcing Americans to pay the highest drug prices in the world while stashing their profits in tax havens overseas, even though most of the medicines they profit from are produced with taxpayer-funded research.

All this, in the self-described wealthiest, strongest and most righteous nation on Earth; all this from politicians, economists and other falsifiers of reality with an obvious fixation on deceptive syntax and zero tolerance for the shameful reality of hunger among their constituents; all this in the name of sacrosanct free enterprise, of the capitalist empire that has steadfastly attacked the welfare state and undermined health- and life-saving assistance programs that sap its profitability.

Trading humanness and reason for right-wing political muscle, a number of would-be presidents hinted recently that anyone who criticizes their vision of reality is a traitor. If treason is to be so defined, I am part of a growing phalanx of fellow defectors who cannot countenance the way the mainstream media, too timid to contest the Orwellian gobble-dygook to which it is treated, allow linguistic perversion to creep up into the popular discourse and choke the truth while ignoring the deafening silence and appalling lethargy of the masses

♦

Fifteen years ago a new century dawned, a new millennium began, full of illusive promises and fanciful auguries. The American Dream, I discovered bit by bit, is a vast exaggeration, a myth invented by and marketed for a privileged and resourceful few who know how to play the game, pull strings, milk the system, and sell themselves to the highest bidder. Once a middle-class society with professed core values of hard work, opportunity, and fair play, the U.S. is now being submerged by a tsunami of cold-blooded reactionary economic, political, and religious influences. The victim of corporate greed, its middle class is frittering away. With the explosive growth of the radical right—fueled by fears generated by economic dislocation and demonizing conspiracy theories that exploit the fears of blue-collar workers and mental Neanderthals—while "Christian" hate groups proliferate and vent their bile on changing racial demographics and, notably, the election of the first African-American president. An angry backlash against what political and religious conservatives perceive as the "socialization" of America has spawned a blind, undifferentiating hatred of Muslims, anti-intellectualism, censorship, racial profiling (with the concomitant rise in police brutality), as well as a form of jingoism that openly condones (or cheers) the use of torture on suspected but unindicted terrorists. Conducted in 2009, a Pew Forum on Religion and Public Life survey revealed that the more Americans go to church, the more prone they are to applaud "extraordinary renditions" and "enhanced interrogation" techniques. There is something odious about people who shut their eyes tight and proclaim the infallibility of their faith while fellow human beings are being tormented and humiliated.

In turn, rabid opposition to same-sex marriage, immigration, the social and cultural advances of non-Caucasians, and the upward mobility of women have bared an image of America that belies its self-view and professed high ideals.

◆

Runaway capitalism is also reinforcing America's incestuous relations with autocratic or marginally democratic regimes around the world and stoking war fever. To keep up the juggernaut's momentum, while doubts over the purpose and direction of conflicts widens, the Pentagon, a rudderless institution, addresses a growing recruitment problem by spending millions of taxpayer dollars on programs designed to deceive, seduce, and capture the youth of America. U.S. conduct at home and abroad is contributing to the mounting suspicion that it talks with a forked tongue and acts solely in its own political and hegemonic interests.

The result of a glut of media-driven mythmaking, the rift between reality and reporting has ended. According to Sonoma University Prof. Peter Phillips, the widening credibility gap has resulted in "a literal truth emergency ... the result of phony elections, illegal preemptive wars, torture camps, doctored intelligence, and issues that intimately impact our lives at home, from healthcare to education." Clearly, this truth emergency stems from the failures of the Fourth Estate to serve as the free and outspoken conscience of America.

◆

A lesser dream exists for those who have nothing left but dreams to sustain them. They all know that what separates them for the greater dream is America itself. They lack America's killer instinct. America is the love child of lofty idealism corrupted by persistent, obsessive sloganeering and the dictates of unrestrained free enterprise. The flag; the Pledge of Allegiance; God's ubiquitous intrusion into affairs of state; an air of coyness and moral superiority; a pugnacious, confrontational streak; an annoying propensity to see itself as stately and righteous—all prop up America's insolent pretense. Shibboleths are carved into America's hide. They help perpetuate an iconic self-image that its actions unfailingly belie. The U.S. may well be the richest, most powerful nation on earth, but it is not the "greatest." America has carved an idealized facsimile of its history that relies on fiction. According to that mythology, America has achieved "greatness" by sheer spunk, ingenuity and toil. It shamelessly ignores the suffering and humiliation of African slaves, whose labor fueled America's financial growth, and it pooh-poohs the unscrupulous treaties forced upon Indigenous Americans whom it very nearly exterminated. Much of America's past is the chronicle of white interlopers whose prosperity hinges on oppression and exploitation. Greatness is an attribute reserved for countries that do not exploit their citizens so that a small elite may thrive.

◆

At this writing, well ahead of the 2016 presidential free-for-all, certain that he alone can mend the dream and bring it to fruition, and without the slightest indication that he can clinch the nomination, let alone be elected, I am pledging my support for a man whose chances are defined by, and contingent on, the national psyche. Alas, I fail to discern in this country the same feelings of outrage that inspired the storming of the Bastille in 1789 or stoked the October Revolution in 1917. Only loud, widespread, persistent indignation can help purge the evil forces that have America in their grip. The U.S. does not resemble the fabled image it has of itself. Perhaps it never did. Worse, in veering steadily to the right, it is degenerating from a pseudo-democracy into a neo-feudal state in which an ever-growing number of vassals will have to struggle so that the lords of capital can live in the style to which they are accustomed. In essence, America has evolved into a Mafia state, both in criminality and in the megalomaniac character of its governance. The two-party system — both parties the flip side of the same tarnished coin, both beholden to Wall Street, both committing larceny on the poor — is a sinister joke. Only an Elliot Ness (or better yet a Robespierre, or a Lenin) could galvanize a sufficient number of Americans into the kind of radical action that forever rid France and Russia of greedy monarchs, a do-nothing aristocracy, venal merchants and a dissolute clergy. Only an unswerving Socialist could help drown out the racist, xenophobic, anti-Semitic and pro-fascist rhetoric that the scoundrels on the right keep spewing.

The man I speak of, Senator Bernie Sanders of Vermont, I believe, desperately wants to put a soul back into a nation that has lost its heart, a nation that seems to favor weirdoes who talk lovingly of walls, watchtowers, weapons and wars, who want to eliminate Social Security, do away with Medicare, Medicaid, unemployment insurance and food stamps, who push for more restrictive voting laws that disenfranchise minorities, and who, like crybabies, threaten to shut down the government while handing the super-rich fat tax breaks.

Senator Sanders' policy goals are not idle promises; they're reminders of what a real democracy must deliver. Candidates for political office are defined by those who vote for them: When white supremacists urge voters to endorse a certain presidential contender, it doesn't take a genius to conclude that the contender champions his supporters' views. Given the current political climate, the increasing popularity of deluded hate mongers, and America's pathological fear of Socialism, I am not optimistic. I find it a sad irony that many

Americans will vote against their interests because the system that makes these benefits possible is called Socialism. While the criminally insane are safely behind bars, the criminally stupid are now crawling out of the woodwork, especially in red states where they are all atwitter at the prospect of turning back the clock and destroying the last vestiges of democracy.

As for God saving the republic, I do not put my faith in an allegorical entity too busy to intervene in human affairs.

It would be useful to remember that sixty million dreams were extinguished during the Second World War. The victor? Fascism. It didn't win on the battlefield. It didn't win right away. It won because the same fictional misgivings, the same avarice, and the same groundless animosity that invigorated it early in the twentieth century never really subsided. The symbols of fascism became anathema, but the causes ... went deep. And gradually, slowly, one step at a time, all those vices, tolerated at first then treated as virtues, are now again being proclaimed as the only acceptable view.

♦

I am not a corporate reporter. I refuse to act as a stenographer for U.S. propaganda. I'll take my chances and speak out. I shall not be silenced, except by force. What will it be? A "freak" accident? A "stray" bullet? A poisoned meal at 33,000 feet above sea level on a flight to Zurich (as happened to a fellow journalist investigating secret links between U.S. and Swiss banks, money laundering schemes and the proceeds from narco-trafficking)? I can see it already: My death will be attributed to "an irreversible cessation of life." Weasel words. The obit will be speckled with calumnies.

Meanwhile, I expect shady politicians to be described as "ethically underfed." Or will honest historians shun euphemisms in favor of such fitting terms as "inept," "avaricious," "corrupt," "deceitful," "usurious," and "morally bankrupt"?

The U.S. has always prided itself on being the world's most prefect democracy. Americans claim the right to meddle in other countries' affairs, often bullying them to embrace American-style democracy. America's obsession with exporting "democracy" is not grounded in altruism; it's inspired by the political and economic kickbacks alliances generate. To no one's surprise the system is flawed, kept alive by shameless sloganeering and underwritten by oligarchs.

Behind the scenes, growing numbers of Americans insist this grand larceny must end, lest they abscond to a parallel but real and expanding universe that views this nation — as does this writer — with rising nausea

Stay tuned.

WHAT NEXT, BOOK BURNINGS?

The First Amendment provides the best legal protection for free expression. As a result, people don't think censorship exists in the United States. Indeed, compared to other countries where journalists are routinely imprisoned, or worse, for alleged libel, sedition or heterodoxy, members of America's Fourth Estate are on a more solid footing.

But this doesn't mean that speech in America is free. Reporters still risk harassment or jail time for refusing to disclose the identity of confidential sources. Or they face censorship (and censure) if their accounts do not harmonize with a publication's "editorial philoso-phy" — doublespeak for "let's not antagonize our subscribers and alienate our advertisers."

In other words, freedom of the press belongs to those who own the presses.

Less extreme but indicative of a typically American form of paranoia, infringements on free speech occur regularly, often well below the radar screen. They dramatically illustrate how embryonic dreams can be disfigured and even aborted before they have a chance to hatch. To wit:

    ℞ A tenth-grader in California was charged with sexual harassment for bringing her copy of Judy Blume's *Forever* to school to lend to a friend.   The friend showed it to an-other student, who read excerpts to a group of children during recess. The teacher confiscated the book and filed charges against the student who'd brought it to school, even though she had not witnessed the reading. The teacher argued that the book was "like a loaded gun."

School administrators backed off the sexual harassment charge but took disciplinary action against the student. The matter was quietly dropped when the National Coalition Against Censorship demanded that the school justify its action. The incident never made the news. The student returned to school as if nothing had ever happened. However, for students aware of the incident, *Forever* will always be associated with the disapproval of school authorities. Kids will think twice before they bring a book to school to lend to a friend. The take-home lesson: Some issues are off limits. You're not supposed to express interest in these issues. And you're forbidden to tell anyone that you do.

Forever was removed from school libraries in a couple of Texas counties. Works by Isabel Allende, Toni Morrison, Richard Wright, Barbara Kingsolver, E. R. Frank, Rodolfo Anaya, and Lois Lowry were also pulled off the shelves in other states. Dozens other titles are being impugned, some for their erotic content, others for challenging dearly held political and religious beliefs.

Such onslaught against academic freedom and free inquiry may not rise to the level of incarceration or retaliatory "fatwa," but the cumulative effect undermines the value placed on reading, on the acquisition of knowledge... and on the dreams these pursuits can spawn. Worse, it creates a framework for a national policy to suppress information deemed "inappropriate," "profane," or "unpatriotic" by certain groups who would, should they be so empowered, rule from the pulpit. Truth, like wayward dreams, they would proclaim, shall not be tolerated.

Efforts to muzzle the press, stifle artistic expression and subvert free thought while stepping up its own deceitful propaganda is being daily turned up a notch with a series of seemingly isolated but incestuously linked initiatives that reflect the right wing's obsession with controlling information—and manipulating the minds of Americans.

Capricious attempts by right-wing ideologues to put a chill on independent inquiry and speculation, freedom of expression, creativity and dissent through the use of blackjack tactics, find fertile ground and continue to manifest themselves in shameful ways:

    ❧ The House of Representatives garnered bipartisan support for a bill that would raise from $32,000 to half a million dollars the top fines for broadcast "indecency." The fines would apply to commentators, talk-show hosts, musicians and filmmakers. Which is worse, a fleeting glimpse of one of Janet Jackson's nipples, a sonorous four-letter expletive or deceptive commentaries and rank disinformation regurgitated by purveyors of right-wing hype?

❧ During an annual Banned Book Week, a Houston-area parent challenged *Fahrenheit 451*, Ray Bradbury's incendiary work about reading and freedom of thought. "It's just all kinds of filth," the parent said, admitting that he had never read the book. Never let fact interfere with opinion.

❧ Calling it "anti-American" and "anti-military," city council members in Lakewood, Colorado, removed an artwork by an Air Force veteran in which he quoted the "irreligious libertine" Ben Franklin's pacifist views.

❧ In a bid to increase its revenues, Google developed "ambient-audio identification technology" that uses personal computers' internal microphones to monitor what television channels Americans watch. The U.S. government was salivating.

❧ Not to be outdone, Microsoft submitted a patent application for a "censoring filter," which would alter digital speech recordings "so that undesired words or phrases are either unintelligible or inaudible."

❧ At a Manchester, New Hampshire, awards dinner honoring defenders of the First

Amendment, featured guest, former Speaker of the House and once-presidential hopeful, Newt Gingrich, proposed "a different set of rules" to govern free speech in light of the war of terror. The terrorist threat, he argued, "will lead us to want to know what is said in every suspect place in the country [and] lead us to learn how to close down every web site that is dangerous." Would that include the ones that chronicle Gingrich's own moral turpitude?

[Could these "different set of rules" be the inspiration of a recent court order demanding that Apple help the Federal Bureau of Investigation bypass the security features of an iPhone recovered from Syed Rizwan Farook, who, along with his wife, killed 14 people last December in San Bernardino, California? At stake is whether the U.S. government can legally compel a company to sabotages its own products in the name of fighting crime, especially when the FBI's assertion that the phone contains valuable evidence is at odds with the known facts of the case].

    ❧ PBS was railroaded into pulling an episode of the children's show, *Postcards from Buster*, when then-Education Secretary Margaret Spellings, an outspoken homophobe, complained that in a certain segment, Buster, a rabbit, learns how sugar maple is made in Vermont at the home of children with two female parents.

&c Local residents in Loveland, Colorado attacked a public sculpture because the figures in it were nude. As a compromise, the Visual Arts Commission moved the work to a less prominent venue. A clear case of the body politic's spurious aversion for the naked truth.

&c In McAllen, Texas, fearing that it would alienate major oil and energy industry contributors, the International Museum of Art and Science removed a sculpture of a globe assembled with gas station signs and mufflers sitting on an oil barrel. Yes, "hypocrisy is the homage that vice pays to virtue."

&c A fourteen-year-old freshman at the Coral Academy of Science in Reno, Nevada, was barred from reciting W. H Auden's classic, *The More Loving One* in the state finals of the Poetry Out Loud contest. Administrators objected to the poem's "profane" language ("damn" and "hell"). Egad!

&c Under fire because of language depicting the realities of racism, and even though it had been taught for ten years, James Collier's historical book, *War Comes to Willy Freeman,* was removed by the principal from a middle school in Ithaca, New York,

   ↲ In Portland, Oregon, Douglas County commissioners asked a museum to remove a display of the pagan goddess Hebe from a historical exhibit. [The rumor that offended parties promptly rallied in church and engaged in idolatrous prayer before a statue of Saint Anthony, beseeching the patron of lost objects to help museum administrators recover their souls is apocryphal].

   ↲ Last December, all schools in rural Greenville, Virginia were shut down "as a precaution," after an Arabic calligraphy assignment triggered angry reactions among some parents who contended that the lesson was meant to convert their children to Islam." Several parents asked that the teacher be dismissed: "She should be fired because she had [them] write an abomination to their faith." The assignment was not meant to promote a religious viewpoint or subvert any religious belief. It merely drew attention to the beauty and elegance of classical Arabic script. Imagine the discomfiture of these ignoramuses if they knew where numbers come from ... or that the father of algebra *(al-jabr)* was a man named Muhammad ibn Musa al-Khwarizmi.

◆

We don't put people in jail for what they write or think—yet. But we might do so if the mind manipulators of the fascist right have their way; if the illiterate philistines to whom they appeal happily support their master plan to keep the masses stupid, unschooled and uninformed. Meanwhile, we grimly influence what they think by monitoring, or criminalizing what they read. Other civilized nations react to this aberration with incredulity, consternation and derision.

"How can this happen in a country which calls itself *'the leader of the free world'* and purports to embrace free speech," a French journalist asked me in the wake of the *Charlie Hebdo* massacre, when the world rose to cheer freedom of expression. I was about to recite a litany of causes, one more vexing than the other, to explain this paradox. Instead, I shrugged and smiled. The question was rhetorical; anyone who asks it already knows the answer. It was the kind of question, very French in texture, one part genuine astonishment, two parts sarcasm, fashioned to discomfit the smug and stump the ill-informed to which I would often resort in my writings. After all, had I not brought to school some sixty years ago an oddball assortment of items for show-and-tell — all carefully selected to astound and shock: my two-headed pet turtle Janus; an exquisitely explicit anatomical atlas; my father's gynecological speculum; and an illustrated copy of one of the Marquis de Sade's works — without incurring the wrath of my teacher or fear that I might bring it upon myself?

Of course, I was about ten at the time and living in France. Now in my seventies, I find it a great and offensive contradiction that a nation that has honed sleaze to an art and wallows in abject promiscuity can be — or pretend to be — so strait-laced when it comes to fornication but so tolerant of government knavery. But that's another story.

♦

According to the Committee to Protect Journalists, scores of newsmen around the world are in prison without having been charged with a crime. Some are being held, incommunicado, by the United States. The U.S. ranks sixth among jailers of journalists, just behind the glorious nation of Uzbekistan, upon which the U.S. lavishes large sums of foreign aid, and whose abysmal human rights record is tied with Myanmar's. Is one still judged by the company one keeps?

In Harrisburg, Virginia, the house of a professor and her family was set on fire, along with the anti-war sign they had displayed. The family was driven from their blazing home for expressing their political views. Denouncing the arson as "domestic terrorism," community members rallied for free speech with signs reading, "I thought this was America." One might wonder whether, disabused, they all moved to Uzbekistan.

Who can forget President George W. Bush's legislation containing provisions advocating political litmus tests for federal science advisory committee nominees and the deliberate distribution of false scientific information? Or his oxymoronic "free speech zones" where people carrying signs opposing his policies are relegated out of sight and hearing of his motorcades — whereas those carrying friendly messages are welcome in the president's vicinity? None is so deaf as he who refuses to hear.

And where were the signs voicing indignation when a Florida court of appeals unanimously agreed with an assertion by Fox News that there is no rule against the distortion and falsification of facts in the U.S.? Are Fox's purveyors of myth and lies taking a page from Lenin: *"A lie told often enough becomes the truth."*?

♦

A First Amendment is not enough. People have to understand it, believe in it and protect it. Freedom of expression is not only a fundamental right; it is an essential aspect of an intellectually emancipated, enlightened and informed society. As for the press, its role is to:

> *"serve no party but the people; [to] be the organ of truth, [to] follow no caucuses but its own convictions; [to] not support the Administration, but criticize it; [to] oppose all frauds and shams wherever and whatever they are; [to] advocate principles and ideas rather than prejudices and partisanship."*[4]

---

[4] *Joseph Pulitzer (1847-1911).*

SO MANY ALTARS, SO LITTLE LOVE

When people decide that one brand of unreality is not weird enough, they fabricate new ones, each nattily tailored to suit divergent but equally aberrant convictions, all apt to inflame passions and ignite sectarian squabbles.

Take the houses of worship that proliferate in and around the small town where I live. They are there in plain sight, stripped of all allegory, like the corner mini-mart, the seedy gas station, the fast-food emporia, the crumbling trailer parks, with their quota of registered sex offenders and parolees, the Joshua trees dying on stretches of a garbage-strewn desert landscape, and the all-night drinking holes. They rise, banal and smug, monuments of idolatry, temples of falsehood and spiritual bondage in whose sanctum sanctorum are manipulated the fears and obsessions and hopes and chimeras that haunt the worshippers. Freedom from dogma (atheism) is anathema, their clerics assert; secularism (the prohibition of religious influence in the determination of state policies) is a damnable sin, they thunder. Jesus is salvation they proclaim; and so sinners and slaves flock to their altars hoping to be unshackled and cleansed.

I don't have to go far to find these sanctuaries. They teem and multiply, while schools decay and close, hospitals go bankrupt, cultural institutions are defunded, and vital social services are slashed in the name of "fiscal restraint," while wickedness and corruption flourish unchecked in council chambers and legislatures across the nation.

There are more altars on this vast barren plateau than parks, playgrounds or bookstores. (One forlorn county library opens only two days a week because the only book most people read in these parts is the Bible). Yet there is very little religion in these holy abodes, only rituals and unbending beliefs and the ironclad conviction by every cult that it alone has the key to God's kingdom.

◆

In my neighborhood, in a three-square-block area, rise five congregations. Their billboards, like movie marquees or roadside election-campaign posters all proclaim to be serving Christ the Redeemer, the Savior, Son of God and King of Kings. All promise grace through Christian fellowship, but their parishioners would rather burn in hell than worship in ecumenical harmony. Catholics will not pray with Baptists; Lutherans and Quakers don't mix. Orthodox and Seventh-Day Adventists can't see eye to eye. Schisms, which began to develop soon after the dawning of Christianity in 325 C.E., some trivial, others titanic, continue to hinder the advent of Christian oneness. It is infinitely easier, and more expedient, to worship the Prince of Peace than to walk in his footsteps. Living by example, freed from coercive codified doctrine, is much harder than submitting to robotic ritual. Which is why the faithful all convene to watch each other sit and stand and kneel and cross themselves and bow their heads and throw trembling hands toward heaven in mindless synchronicity. Codified imitation reinforces the illusion of harmony and commonness of purpose among men. The fervency of their performance earns them the sham esteem of their fellow worshippers and, provisionally the clean conscience they crave. They love their "neighbor" to glorify their own ego. Their love does not include self-sacrifice. Homo sapiens are seduced by histrionics. We respond to gestures, not reason.

On Sundays, arrayed in their glad rags, pious souls spill out of freshly waxed cars and gather in solemn formations in their respective shrines. There, they pray in vacant-eyed monotones or, fired up by paroxysms of trance-like jubilation, they swing to and fro and chant words so often uttered that they have been stripped of all meaning.

They all insist that humankind needs religion, that we are incapable of shepherding our own destiny, that God is the alpha and omega, the promise and the reward. Their convictions are so firmly held and so bereft of common sense that they see no contradiction between the "immanent" deity they worship and the invisible, deaf, voiceless, and hard-hearted —

but almighty—spirit so disengaged from the lives of his master work that he (or she?) is never moved by the calamities that befall them, the dreams that elude them.

So immersed are they in their devotions that they can't abide the notion that religion, which turns hoaxes into articles of faith, divides people and pits them against one another, that it ignores some, shuns others, that it is exclusionary, despotic, self-absorbed, and intolerant, that the Golden Rule applies to the "others" among *us*, not the "others" among *them*, that much blood has been shed in its name, that torrents continue to be spilled while men engage in one-way conversations with a God that cannot hear, that ignores men's dreams and never sheds a tear.

◆

The dogmas of religion are kept deviously simple and few in numbers, forced tersely and without commentary: "Thou shalt." "Thou shalt not." Religion punishes the present to expiate the future.

Those who distinguish between civil and religious intolerance are deceiving themselves and misleading others. Both forms of bigotry are inseparable. It is impossible to coexist with those we consider profane, impure, damned, or "different;" heretics must be exorcised or slain.

Favoring tyranny, religions preach only servitude and submission. Religious fanatics are the storm troopers of their creeds. The dreams they peddle are not of this world.

One of the tools dream busters use to promote their own vision of reality is deception. The quarrels that cleave society stem from the frenzied tug-of-war between conflicting ideas. Essential truths are trampled in the process. Everyone has beliefs, convictions, and worldviews. Many of our perceptions are erected on a vast scaffolding of dogmas and fictions — usually someone else's. Keen on cramming children's dormant brain cells, parents force-feed their own opinions, imprint their own idiosyncrasies and bestow their own delusions, and children cling to them indiscriminately, later falsely claiming that they are the offspring of their own cogitations because they encourage them not to think, because they shield them from what they fear most — the bewildering ambiguities of perceived reality — because they keep them warm and cozy in their self-spun ideological cocoons.

♦

Man is fated to ponder his morality. His dignity depends on it. Every human being must endure the conflict between otherworldliness and selfishness. He can avoid neither; such is the paradox of morality: How to live knowing we are accountable for the crimes of our century? How to silence the dreams in which the cries of the martyrs can be heard? Must we choose between infinity without existence or a finite existence? The world cannot be healed without the dream. Every action is sealed in time, irretrievable, unforgettable. That is the essence of human suffering—no compensation, no redemption. Great decisions need to be made in the glow of momentary blindness, in the din of deafness.

Man is in a state of house arrest; he is the galley slave of temporality. Every moment is as heavy as the sum total of our world's history. He must once and for all consult his reason rather than yield to his instincts.

THE DREAM ASCENDING

Ibegan this narrative by professing an early fascination for the truth. I also stated my belief that the truth (the inconvenient kind), a non-negotiable commodity upon which freedom and justice depend, must be vigilantly tracked and swiftly exposed — consequences be damned. Diluted by specious reasoning, undermined by baseless but dearly held convictions, or distorted by misinformation, the truth is a fragile artifact. If baring it is a challenge, acknowledging it without hesitation in its irreducible nudity can be harrowing for those habituated to comforting myths and misrepresentations; it will forever change their lives. Owing the truth's asymmetric complexion, its transitory, uneven, and idiosyncratic character, the quest to distill from it some inalienable reality is a fool's errand. There are more truths than there are lies, most of them no less deceptive than the falsehoods with which they compete:

Virtual truth, like virtual sightseeing or virtual sex, is an incongruity.

An *implied* truth, often an oblique lie and the tool of politicians, is based on inference, and manipulated to deliver palatable fibs — not fact.

An *apparent* truth is like a mirage; it has no basis in reality but it dazzles those in search of fictitious oases.

A *subjective* truth is what is true about one's particular experience of the world. It lends credence to the proposition that reality is what the self perceives, but it overlooks the possibility that perceptions (like mirages) can betray the perceiver. Though there is some truth in them, appearances are *not* the truth.

Ignorance or chicanery yields *partial* or *half*-truths. These are rose-tinted truths delivered in such a way as to obscure the *whole* truth. Politicians, business magnates, and military strategists are notorious purveyors of half-truths.

Without empirical validation, a *potential* truth is a useless hypothesis.

Existing beyond human comprehension, *unimaginable* truths, the fantasies on which religious doctrine is grounded, can never be fathomed because they obscure *unbearable* truths.

Gospel truth rests on blind faith, not demonstrable fact, and the "good news" it purports to spread is false and deceitful.

The only truth that matters is the *plain truth*. *Plain* truths are buttressed by their irrefutability, their conformity to fact: two plus two equals four; water is two parts hydrogen, one part oxygen; the Earth revolves around the Sun. The *plain* truth is the bane of doctrinaires; hard as they try, they can't disprove or distort them. It is the most harmful of all truths because it is the truth men fear most. People don't want to be lulled into states of self-awareness. Reality is too much to bear. Once grasped, it rips to shreds the ideological cocoons in which they take refuge. Human nature denatures the truth. It is the chief impediment to harmony among the species.

♦

I then proceeded to suggest that we are never quite as free to contemplate the truth—and to exalt it—as when we dream; that dreaming is the purest manifestation of inner freedom. I added that the *Dreamdom* is the culmination of our unerring yearning for liberty and justice, for love and compassion, for wisdom and enlightenment, not a cornucopia of material delights. To live is not to bask in self-satisfaction, revel in comfort or wallow in pleasure, but to selflessly acknowledge that all living beings are irreplaceable, that they have intrinsic rights that cannot be abrogated. Such ethos is not found in the soothing platitudes of religion, the dizzying abstractions of metaphysics or the reactionary flimflam of neo-liberalism. Life is a rehearsal, not an improvisation.

I also proposed that once fulfilled, the *Dreamdom* would allow us to live without expecting anything, that it would empower us not to tarry in the present, not to linger in our memories, not to rush toward the future, but to anchor ourselves in our consciousness of ourselves.

Last, I catalogued a number of obstacles— evils (the list is far from exhaustive)— that must be overcome in order to craft a world free from bondage and ignorance, prejudice and hatred, poverty and hunger, greed and corruption, cruelty and war. It will take another book, far more ambitious than this diminutive volume to catalogue the lies and bestial deeds that imperil a nascent *Dreamdom.* The future is unpredictable. Its unpredictability has since acquired an apocalyptic character. A pervasive culture of fear threatens dreamers, sapping their ability to dream freely. It has become unsafe to dream because dreaming involves asking inconvenient questions that lead to unambiguous answers and beg for painful solutions:

Imagine a realm in which corporate interests are not allowed to jeopardize the well-being of the citizenry, in which efforts by financial institutions and religious entities to suborn the body politic and subjugate the masses are not tolerated. Think of a society that abolishes statutes that circumvent laws enacted to stop environmental degradation. Picture a culture that reverses the vicious cycle of wealth and power that leads to poverty and disenfranchisement by making the world safe from predatory capitalism. Envision a citizenry that does not impose its standards of morality on others; that does not procreate without considering the land's ability to sustain their offspring; that pledges to prevent the genetic alteration of foods and the adulteration of crops by exposure to toxic chemicals; that will scrap nuclear weapons, use public funds to repave roads, shore up crumbling bridges, build affordable housing, invest in schools and hospitals, and erect cultural centers dedicated to enlightenment. Think about a community of like-minded individuals who honor the proletariat for they toil so some of us can keep enjoying the lifestyle to which we think we are entitled. Picture a civilization that makes no idols of celebrities whose only claim to fame is their celebrity, many of them mediocre human beings who but for their height, brawn or dubious sex appeal, would be living in obscurity instead of earning obscene wages. Visualize a nation-state that has no other gods before it but knowledge, truth, wisdom and compassion.

◆

There is ample cause to ask whether profound discontent among the poor, the disenfranchised, and the downtrodden is not, in great part, responsible for the ignoble violence to which they sometimes resort. Misery, despair and persecution can lead good men to do evil. Is a woman who steals bread to feed a hungry child a criminal? Does a man whose plot of land is commandeered at the point of a gun, whose fruit trees are stripped bare, whose groves are turned to ashes, and whose domicile is bulldozed by hostile intruders, have the moral right to rebel? Don't people subjected to humiliation or who are relentlessly tormented because of their race, color, religion or social status, have the moral obligation to strike back?

Jean-Jacques Rousseau was right. Despite the infamies leveled against him by monarchists, the Church, and social conservatives, he had the inspiration — and the temerity — to reject the odious concept of "original sin" and to propose that although man is born free he is everywhere in chains, that he comes into this world pure-hearted and that society renders him evil. (I reject his claim that man can be both free and ruled as a contradiction. We can be truly free only when we govern ourselves, when we manage our own dreams without intruding on the dreams of others).

"Universal evil" is a Judeo-Christian falsehood whose only goal is to rationalize, and punish, ex-post-facto, human foibles. No one suggests that a shark is "mean" or that a lamb is "gentle," that a scorpion is "wicked" whereas a butterfly is virtuous. We accept, without commentary, their individual temperament as a reflection of the roles nature calls upon them to play. Surely, Homo sapiens is an imperfect (or unfinished) "creation" capable of all manner of dirty deeds. But we must also ask ourselves to what extent education, religion, exposure to the cultural milieu in which we live, and the socio-political and economic structures erected without our direct consent influence our thoughts, actions and dreams.

♦

The evil of our age is the existential malaise, the melancholy, the cunning "angst" that stalk us at every turn. Dissonance is modern man's predicament. I always knew that evil exists — how can one be alive and not recognize it — and I acknowledged its existence in my other works as one of the ineluctable realities of the human condition. Evil, like the truth, has many faces. Evil is the beating that my father endured at the hands of his Gestapo captors; I was three when I saw it happen. I still bear the scars, unholy, unhealed, this spectacle carved on my soul. Evil is the death by starvation, exhaustion and murder, of nine tenths of my family at Auschwitz and Dachau and Bergen-Belsen, as is the slaughter of millions of their brethren in Hitler's extermination camps. Evil is the massacre of more than a million Armenians less than half a century earlier; evil is Turkey's unwillingness to confess to the crime. Evil is the summary execution in a small French village of ten veterans of the "Great War" in retaliation for the assassination of a German officer who was screwing the baker's daughter; I was six when I witnessed the gruesome scene. I remember fixating on the rivulets of blood that oozed from their lifeless bodies, pooled onto the rain-slick sidewalk and cascaded into the gutter. I was five. Evil is the saturation bombardments by the Allies of dozens of cities during which tens of thousands of innocent lives were snuffed. Evil is the transformation — overnight — of unfaltering fascists into loyal "communists" when the Axis fell and the Russians stormed the Balkans. Evil is the inspiration that drove our Jerusalem neighbors to gang up on my parents for allowing me to befriend a Palestinian girl. We were both thirteen. Evil are religious fanaticism and manic nationalism. Evil is the strategic and systematic dispossession and dehumanization of the Palestinian people by Jewish zealots whose memory of history has conveniently faded. Evil is colonialism and slavery and ghettoization. Evil are the lies that justify illegal, immoral and unwinnable wars. Evil are the millionaires who influence every aspect of life, who control education, manipulate the media, fix prices, regulate farming, establish fiscal strategies, influence elections, and manipulate foreign policy. Evil is the avoidance of genuine dialogue between adversaries; it is one of the worst failings of diplomacy and part of a wider refusal to listen to others viewed as enemies. Evil are governments that assign monetary values to human life. Evil is capitalism, a social and economic system ruled by a small clique of mercenaries who buy and corrupt elected officials, who steal from the poor to give to the rich. And evil—the evil of stupidity—are the masses that, instead of rebelling against their tormentors, surrender to social and psychological paralysis.

Evil (like "God" or the "Messiah,") does not have a "nature." It's a concept, not an entity. It exists and expresses itself in ways that mirror the diseased imagination and cruelty of those who inflict it. To dissect it, to analyze its myriad faces is to belittle it.

♦

Depending on their predilections and sense of history, all humans think they are born too early or too late. Unlike our best friends — dogs — who live in the moment and whose sole purpose in life is to please us, we are never satisfied with the era through which we pass. We always want to change something, reset the clock, make it run faster, retard its course. We foolishly believe in a myth called "the good old days" and we bank our dreams on a future we can neither predict nor postpone. We can only deal with the present, as we grow older at our own pace, in our own time. It's a roll of the dice.

♦

Time flies at dizzying speeds and Earth spins but never looks over its shoulders to see the harm men do to it or the great evils to which they succumb. I smell war in the air. It's an old familiar scent, part sulfur, part blood. The media talk about it in vague, counterfactual terms; they use the conditional tense, as if euphemisms and qualifiers are enough to prevent it. In my own backyard, a large number of people, most of who react to crises by preaching violence, use Orwellian language and lick their chops at the prospect of "bombing the shit out of the enemy," while twenty million of their fellow citizens live at or below the poverty line and five hundred thousand children go to bed hungry at night. These statistics haven't prevented certain presidential hopefuls from pledging to abolish social safety nets that allow millions of households to survive in an economy that coddles large corporations and pampers billionaires. The middle class, once the barometer of a healthy, progressive society, is frittering away. Unions, targets of predatory capitalistic policies that keep the working class in their crosshairs, are moribund.

Conscience may be sidestepped, even flouted, but it never deludes.

◆

I face my reality and I bare my dreams in everything I do, say, and write, mindful that candor can be unpalatable (though I bask in the tremors my irreverence causes), aware that it will spark caustic ripostes and bitter denunciations (and exulting in them). My reputation is based on what my detractors say about me. I can't thank them enough.

Evolution may be nature's way of refining our congenital imperfections but it dawdles, it drags its feet, it vacillates. Sometimes, it seems to be running in reverse, suggesting that the human brain may have reached its saturation point, that beyond it lurks irreversible madness.

The status quo is a perpetual motion nightmare from which we must awaken, or it will extinguish our dreams. We keep looking for ourselves in the cosmos's endless void and finding nothing but billions of sepulchers in which our fancies are entombed. There is no one else out there. Humankind is a unique and unrepeatable biological phenomenon forever destined to ponder the enigma of its absurd existence. The mission of sane men is not to reach for the stars but to strive toward refinement through reformation. We shall never ascend to the Dreamdom unless we make a left turn, arm the powerless, infuriate the money-eyed elites, subdue the mighty, and agitate, agitate, agitate. There can be no meaningful revolution without a revolution.

ACKNOWLEDGMENTS

I am indebted to my late parents, learned, urbane, open-minded and progressive, for instilling a love of books and an appreciation for music, art and philosophy, for sparing me the enslavement of religious indoctrination, and for enduring, if not always endorsing, my wildest antics. To my mother, a selfless, unassuming woman of exceptional culture and refinement, I owe my fondness for beauty and symmetry, as well as my reverence for nature. From my father, a loving, iron-willed and incorruptible man who abhorred ostentation and pretense, I learned that self-esteem and a respect for truth bestow infinitely greater rewards than money or prestige.

I salute my teachers, those I pleased and those I exasperated. Their erudition, pedagogical skills and saintly patience for the indolent, unfocused, mercurial and rebellious student I was helped lay the foundations on which I would erect a lifetime career of endless beginnings.

I can never adequately acknowledge the immense influence a number of writers, poets and philosophers have had on the endlessly evolving person I would become and, by extension, on the ideas I would champion or reject. Their prose, verses, insights and eye-opening reflections resonate as intensely today as they did in the days of my youth. Many were French. Of these, one was denied a Christian burial for penning vitriolic anti-religious tracts; five were imprisoned — one for denouncing the brutality of colonialism; the other for suggesting that the blind can be taught to read through the sense of touch; the third, the son of a prostitute, for vagabondage, lewd acts and "other offenses against public decency;" the fourth for stretching the limits of literary freedom in works that mixed raw eroticism with civil disobedience. The fifth spoke

for the common man and spoke out with un-
common bravery against government and military corruption.

My other gurus wrote in Arabic, English,
Dutch, German, Russian, Sanskrit and Span-
ish. Three hailed from Ireland (one of them
did not survive the spurious puritanism of his
Victorian milieu). One died insane, as do
many who seek shelter from the battering
storm of reality in the haven of delirium. One
was anathemized by his own people for at-
tempting to resolve the conflict between religious and secular knowledge, and for depart-
ing from prevailing Aristotelian thought by
emphasizing the limits to human knowledge.
All were freethinkers, now long dead, but
whose iconoclasm and the reformist ideas they
impart still inspire new generations of dreamers.

GLOSSARY

ALLIANCE: *In politics the union of two crooks whose hands are so deeply buried in each other's pockets that they're incapable of robbing a third.*

BEGGAR: *Someone who once relied on his friends.*

BOMB: *Device used to redraw borders.*

BORDER: *In geopolitics, an artificial line between two regions, which separates the imaginary rights of one from the fictitious claims of the other.*

BRAIN: *Organ that allows humans to believe that they are capable of thought.*

CAPITALISM: *Malignant, self-replicating cannibalistic organism that feeds on the scraps it spits out.*

CLEAN CONSCIENCE: *Faulty memory.*

CONVICTION: *Inflexible belief, generally borrowed, usually absurd.*

CYNICISM: *Ability to see things as they really are.*

DEMOCRACY: *Self-defeating system that tolerates the existence of undemocratic institutions.*

DESPOT: *Statesman who turns to tyranny when threatened by justifiable rebellion.*

DREAM: *Strong, enduring yearning to be freed from senseless beliefs and rid of ruthless monarchs, fickle laws, dogmatism, stupidity, mediocrity and war.*

DREAMDOM: *Realm, as yet out of reach, where the DREAM can flourish.*

DREAMER: *One who lives by the DREAM.*

FAITH: *The illogical belief in the occurrence of the impossible.*

FELLOW MAN: *Mythical being we are told to love as ourselves who habitually makes us regret our benevolence.*

JOURNALISM: *First draft of history.*

JUSTICE: *What goes down the drain when doing the "right thing" threatens special interests.*

KILL: *To create an opening without naming a successor.*

LOYALTY: *Virtue of those who haven't yet been betrayed.*

NEUTRALITY: *Crime of indifference; aloofness further debased by cowardice and opportunism.*

OPINION: *Second-hand conviction often modified when circumstances demand.*

PATIENCE: *Waste of time.*

PATRIOT: *Flag-draped narrow-minded xenophobic hooligan.*

PEACE: *Brief, half-hearted intermission between wars.*

PRAGMATISM: *In politics, the desertion of one's principles in favor of a self-serving transaction.*

REVOLUTION: *Inevitable aftermath in a world tyrannized by senseless beliefs, fickle laws, ruthless monarchs, dogmatism, stupidity, mediocrity and war.*

TRUTH: *Insufferable fact or ignominious lie in which we can believe because it invites us not to think.*

UNFREE: *Condition that afflicts those who are prevented from attaining the DREAM.*

Born in Paris, educated in Europe and the Middle East, W. E. Gutman is a retired journalist, a former writer and editor at the late-great New York City-based futurist monthly magazine, *OMNI* and the co-founder of a now defunct military intelligence journal. He reported from Central America from 1994 to 2006, focusing on politics and human rights. He has contributed hundreds of articles, news analyses and editorials to various mainstream and special interest publications. He is the author of ten books, this being his eleventh. He lives with his wife in southern California's "high desert."